# Caderno do Futuro

A evolução do caderno



# LÍNGUA INGLESA

Book 4

ENSINO FUNDAMENTAL

3ª edição
São Paulo - 2013

IBEP

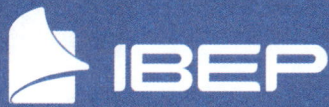

Coleção Caderno do Futuro
Língua Inglesa
© IBEP, 2013

| | |
|---|---|
| **Diretor superintendente** | Jorge Yunes |
| **Gerente editorial** | Célia de Assis |
| **Editor** | Angelo Gabriel Rozner |
| **Assistente editorial** | Fernanda dos Santos Silva |
| **Revisão** | André Odashima |
| | Rachel Prochoroff |
| **Coordenadora de arte** | Karina Monteiro |
| **Assistente de arte** | Marilia Vilela |
| | Nane Carvalho |
| | Carla Almeida Freire |
| **Coordenadora de iconografia** | Maria do Céu Pires Passuello |
| **Assistente de iconografia** | Adriana Neves |
| | Wilson de Castilho |
| **Ilustrações** | José Luís Juhas |
| **Produção gráfica** | José Antônio Ferraz |
| **Assistente de produção gráfica** | Eliane M. M. Ferreira |
| **Projeto gráfico** | Departamento de Arte Ibep |
| **Capa** | Departamento de Arte Ibep |
| **Editoração eletrônica** | N-Publicações |

**CIP-BRASIL. CATALOGAÇÃO-NA-FONTE**
**SINDICATO NACIONAL DOS EDITORES DE LIVROS, RJ**

K38i
3.ed.

Keller, Victoria
 Língua Inglesa : book 4, (9º ano) / Victoria Keller, pseudônimo dos autores Antonio de Siqueira e Silva, Rafael Bertolin. - 3. ed. - São Paulo : IBEP, 2013.
 il. ; 28 cm     (Caderno do futuro)

 ISBN 978-85-342-3571-6 (aluno) - 978-85-342-3575-4 (mestre)

 1. Língua inglesa (Ensino fundamental) - Estudo e ensino.
I. Título. II. Série.

12-8686.        CDD: 372.6521
                CDU: 373.3.016=111

27.11.12  03.11.12                    041071

3ª edição - São Paulo - 2013
Todos os direitos reservados.

Av. Alexandre Mackenzie, 619 - Jaguaré
São Paulo - SP - 05322-000 - Brasil - Tel.: (11) 2799-7799
www.editoraibep.com.br editoras@ibep-nacional.com.br

CTP, Impressão e Acabamento IBEP Gráfica

# SUMÁRIO

## CONTENTS

| | |
|---|---|
| GENERAL REVIEW | 4 |
| LESSON 1 – IRREGULAR VERBS | 20 |
| LESSON 2 – HOW MANY BOOKS DID YOU BUY? | 28 |
| LESSON 3 – I HAVE SOME FRIENDS | 37 |
| LESSON 4 – I DON'T HAVE MUCH MONEY | 45 |
| LESSON 5 – COMPARATIVE DEGREE | 49 |
| REVIEW | 54 |
| LESSON 6 – SUPERLATIVE | 59 |
| LESSON 7 – PRESENT PERFECT TENSE | 66 |
| LESSON 8 – FUTURE TENSE | 75 |
| LESSON 9 – CONDITIONAL TENSE | 82 |
| LESSON 10 – PASSIVE VOICE | 89 |
| LESSON 11 – QUESTION TAGS | 94 |
| LESSON 12 – PRONOUNS | 98 |
| LESSON 13 – GERUND | 106 |
| ADDITIONAL TEXTS | 109 |
| LIST OF IRREGULAR VERBS | 123 |
| GENERAL VOCABULARY | 126 |

**SUBJECT**

**NAME**

**TEACHER**

| HOUR | MONDAY | TUESDAY | WEDNESDAY | THURSDAY | FRIDAY | SATURDAY | SUNDAY |
|---|---|---|---|---|---|---|---|
| | | | | | | | |
| | | | | | | | |
| | | | | | | | |
| | | | | | | | |
| | | | | | | | |
| | | | | | | | |

**TESTS AND WORKS**

# General review

**PLURAL OF NOUNS – Remember:**
Regra geral: acrescenta-se **s** ao singular (pencil, pencil**s**).
Palavras terminadas em **s**, **ch**, **sh**, **o**, **x**, **z**: acrescenta-se **es**.
Palavras terminadas em **y** precedido de vogal: acrescenta-se **s** (boy, boy**s**).
Se o **y** for precedido de consoante, mudará para **ies** (city, cit**ies**).
Palavras terminadas em **man** fazem o plural em **men** (fireman, fire**men**).
Observe estes plurais: foot: **feet**; tooth: **teeth**; goose: **geese**; mouse: **mice**; people (pessoas, povo): **peoples** (povos).
Palavras terminadas em **f** ou **fe** fazem o plural em **ves**: leaf: lea**ves**; thief: thie**ves**.

**1.** Passe para o plural.

a) dog –

b) class –

c) watch –

d) beach –

e) door –

f) window –

g) match –

h) dress –

i) hat –

j) school –

k) bus –

l) kiss –

m) box –

n) fox –

o) wish –

p) child –

q) tooth –

r) foot –

s) lady –

t) baby –

u) leaf –

v) city –

w) activity –

x) toy –

**2.** Complete a cruzadinha escrevendo o plural de:

1. church
2. lady
3. dress
4. kiss
5. tooth
6. bus
7. mouse
8. sister
9. box
10. goose
11. woman
12. tomato
13. knife
14. child
15. foot
16. leaf
17. school

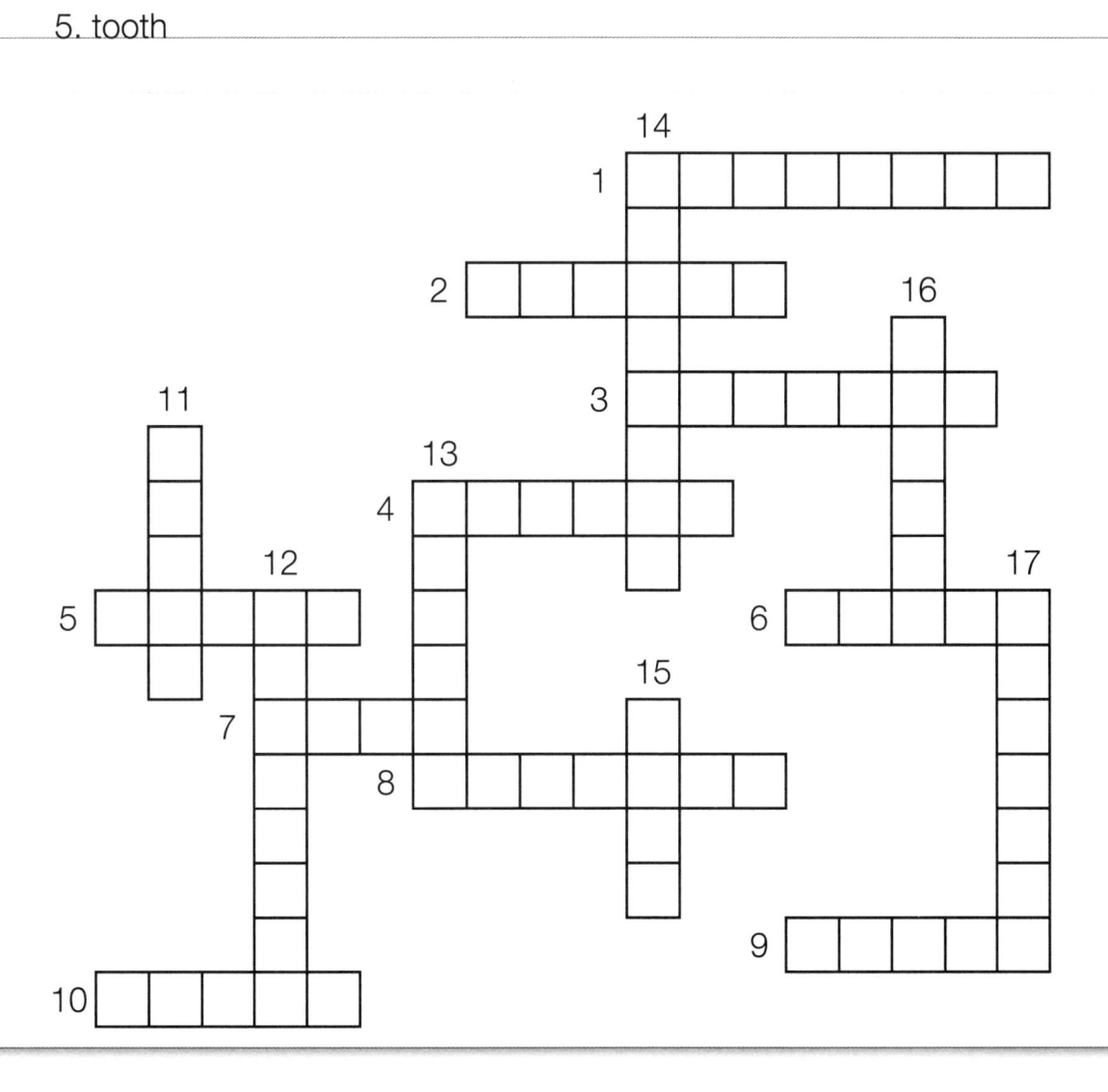

**3.** Mude as palavras em destaque para o plural e faça as adaptações que se fizerem necessárias. Observe o exemplo.

**This** is my friend.
**These are my friends.**

a) This **book** is mine.

b) **I** am well today.

c) **She** likes you.

d) **That** pencil belongs to Jane.

e) The **girl** does her homework.

f) The **child** is beautiful.

g) **He** is playing football.

h) The **tomato** is red.

i) The **bus** is late.

j) **He** was here last month.

k) **This** book is yours.

> **Observação:**
> Os verbos, em geral, terminam por **-s** ou **-es** na terceira pessoa do singular do indicativo presente. Neste caso, o **-s** ou **-es** não indicam plural.

**4.** Escreva as frases na 3ª pessoa do singular. Observe o exemplo.

I like History. (She)
**She likes History.**

a) They teach English. (He)

b) You wash the plants. (He)

c) I speak English. (She)

d) They go to school by bus. (Mary)

e) We catch the ball. (The goalkeeper)

f) I need your help. (She)

g) The birds fly in the sky. (The bird)

h) They do their homework. (She)

i) The babies are hungry. (The baby)

j) I sit near Paul. (She)

k) I carry Mary's bags. (John)

**5.** Complete as frases com adjetivos possessivos.

a) Peter usually goes to school with _____ sister.

b) I enjoy _____ History classes very much.

c) Jane and _____ brother study in the same class.

d) Paul and Mary do _____ homework together.

e) _____ first name is Richard.

f) Mrs Gates loves _____ children very much.

g) Most parents love _____ children.

h) Do you do _____ homework in the morning?

i) Mary is writing a letter to _____ parents.

j) Bob and Jim like _____ country.

k) Charles doesn't like _____ school.

l) The cat didn't eat _____ food.

m) Mary is wearing _____ new dress.

n) I always help _____ mother at home.

**6.** Substitua as palavras em destaque pelo pronome pessoal oblíquo correspondente. Observe os exemplos

I saw Mary in the street yesterday.
I saw her in the street yesterday.
(British English)
I saw Mary on the street yesterday.
I saw her on the street yesterday.
(American English)

a) Peter sent **Flavia** some flowers.

b) I go to work with **John and Fred** every day.

c) Put **the book** on the table.

d) I saw **the President** on TV last night.

e) Put **the money** in a bank.

f) You can go with **Jane** to the party.

g) I told **the teachers** about the accident.

h) Do you speak to **the tourists** in English?

i) Did you meet **your friends** at the party?

j) I wrote **your telephone number** in my notebook.

**7.** Traduza o texto.

Fred is a waiter. He works for a big restaurant. He takes food and drink to people. Fred likes his job very much.

**8.** Relacione os profissionais aos seus respectivos trabalhos.

a) A cook
b) A dentist
c) A driver
d) A policeman
e) A hairdresser
f) A doctor
g) A writer
h) A carpenter
i) A clerk
j) An engineer
k) A farmer
l) A reporter

( ) drives cars, buses...
( ) cuts women's hair.
( ) cooks food.
( ) treats our teeth.
( ) looks after your health.
( ) writes texts, books.
( ) makes furniture.
( ) arrests thieves.
( ) interviews people.
( ) sells things in shops.
( ) builds houses, bridges...
( ) works in a farm.

**9.** Coloque 's somente quando se trata de escritório, consultório ou estabelecimento comercial. Observe o exemplo.

You are not well. Go to the **doctor's**.

a) Can you go to the butcher to buy some meat?
b) You can buy medicines at the chemist   .
c) You can buy vegetables at the grocer   .
d) You can buy flowers at the florist   .
e) You can buy fish at the fishmonger   .

**10.** Responda às perguntas. Observe o exemplo.

What does a bookseller sell?
**A book seller sells books, magazines.**

a) What does a greengrocer sell?

b) What does a florist sell?

c) What does a baker sell?

d) What does a fishmonger sell?

e) What does a chemist sell?

f) What does a newsagent sell?

g) What does a butcher sell?

h) What does a jeweller sell?

**11.** Complete as frases com **sells** ou **does not sell**. Observe o exemplo.

The butcher **does not sell** flowers.
The butcher **sells** meat.

a) The chemist _____ books.
b) The chemist _____ medicine.
c) The fishmonger _____ fish.
d) The fishmonger _____ cakes.
e) The baker _____ bread.
f) The baker _____ meat.

**12.** Leia o texto com atenção, consulte o vocabulário no final do livro e traduza-o para o português.

**AN INTERVIEW**

**Reporter:** Excuse me, who are you?
**Robert:** I'm Robert. Robert Peterson.
**Reporter:** How old are you, Mr Peterson?
**Robert:** I'm thirty years old.
**Reporter:** What's your occupation?
**Robert:** I was unemployed. But now I'm going to work for a travel agency.
**Reporter:** Where is the travel agency, Mr Peterson?
**Robert:** It's near the post office.
**Reporter:** When are you going to begin your new job?
**Robert:** Tomorrow morning, at nine.
**Reporter:** Mr Peterson, why are you going to work in a travel agency?
**Robert:** It's a nice job and I like it very much.
**Reporter:** Thank you, Mr Peterson. Goodbye!
**Robert:** Goodbye.

**13.** Leia o texto abaixo com atenção.

**The meals**
**Breakfast** is at seven in the morning.
**Lunch** is at one in the afternoon.
**Tea** is at four o'clock in the afternoon.
**Dinner** is at seven in the evening.

Agora, marque a alternativa correta.

a) ( ) Breakfast is in the evening.
    ( ) Breakfast is in the morning.
    ( ) Breakfast is in the afternoon.

b) ( ) Lunch is at six o'clock.
    ( ) Lunch is at one o'clock.
    ( ) Lunch is at five o'clock.

**14.** Responda de acordo com o texto.

a) When is breakfast?

b) When is lunch?

c) When is dinner?

d) Traduza para o português.

meals:

breakfast:

lunch:

tea:

dinner:

**15.** Marque a alternativa correta.

a)

( ) It's seven o'clock.
( ) It's eight o'clock.
( ) It's nine o'clock.

b)

( ) It's ten past eight.
( ) It's five past eight.
( ) It's two past eight.

c)

( ) It's a quarter past eight.
( ) It's twenty-five past eight.
( ) It's twenty past eight.

d)

( ) It's twenty-five past eight.
( ) It's half past eight.
( ) It's twenty past eight.

e)

( ) It's a quarter past eight.
( ) It's half past eight.
( ) It's twenty past eight.

f)

( ) It's twenty to nine.
( ) It's ten to nine.
( ) It's a quarter to nine.

g)

( ) It's twenty past eight.
( ) It's ten to nine.
( ) It's a quarter to nine.

**16.** Coloque os ponteiros de acordo com a hora indicada abaixo dos relógios.

a) It is half past nine.

b) It is ten to ten.

c) It is a quarter past ten.

d) It is ten past ten.

e) It is twenty to two.

f) It is a quarter to nine.

g) It is five past nine.

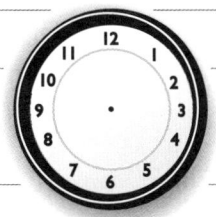

h) It is ten o'clock.

i) It is ten past ten.

**17.** Traduza os diálogos. Emprego do verbo **to do**.

a) – Do you like to sing?
– Yes, I do.
– Do you like to work?
– No, I don't.

b) – Do you like to read?
– Yes, I do.
– Do you like to write?
– No, I don't.

c) – Do you like to hug?
– Yes, I do.
– Do you like to kiss?
– Yes, I do.

**18.** Complete os diálogos abaixo.

a) – Do you like fish?
– No,

– Do you like spinach?
– No,

– What do you like then?
– I like

b) – Do you like music?
– Yes,

– Do you like to dance?
– No,

c) – Does she like coffee?
– No,

– Does she like tea?
– Yes,

d) – Do you want to play football?
   – No,

   – How about volleyball?
   – I hate

   – What do you want to play?
   – I want to play

e) – Do your parents like to listen to the radio?
   – No,

   – Do they like to watch television?
   – Yes,

   – How about you?
   – I hate

**19.** Escreva a pergunta que corresponde à resposta. Observe o exemplo.

– **Do you like bananas?**
– Yes, I like bananas.

a)
   – Yes, she helps her mother.

b)
   – Yes, I wash the plates.

c)
   – Yes, she washes the dishes after meals.

d)
   – Yes, I make my bed every day.

e)
   – Yes, they make their beds every day.

p)
   – Yes, they work on Saturdays.

**20.** Siga o exemplo e escreva os diálogos.
(fish – chicken)
– Do you like fish?
– No, I don't. I prefer chicken.

a) (soup – salad)

b) (steak – rice and eggs)

c) (cake – ice cream)

**21.** Siga o exemplo e escreva os diálogos.

(she lives in Brazil – Portugal)
– **Does she live in Brazil?**
– **No, she doesn't. She lives in Portugal.**

a) (he plays football – tennis)

b) (the teacher lives in a house – flat)

c) (Mary likes Mathematics – History)

d) (coffee – tea)

**22.** Mude as frases para a forma negativa. Observe o exemplo.

**They go to school.**
**They don't go to school.**

a) We study English.

b) She likes salad.

c) They hate fish.

d) My mother cooks well.

e) He eats chicken.

f) My brother likes potatoes.

**23.** Mude as frases para a forma interrogativa. Observe o exemplo.

The children liked the clown.
**Did the children like the clown?**

a) They decided to go to the party.

b) She arrived at six o'clock.

c) The children played tennis yesterday.

d) John borrowed a lot of money from the bank.

e) She remembered my name.

f) They moved to a new house.

g) Mary lived in Canada last year.

**24.** Mude as frases para a forma interrogativa. Observe o exemplo.

John came to class late.
**Did John come to class late?**

a) They knew my teacher.

b) They went to school.

c) They bought a new car last week.

d) She began a new course last month.

e) They drank whiskey at the party.

f) They found the documents in a coffee shop.

**25.** Mude as frases para a forma negativa. observe o exemplo.

John came to class late.
**John didn't come to class late.**

a) They went to school.

b) We knew the lesson.

c) He bought the house.

**26.** Ligue os sinônimos (connect the synonims).

| | |
|---|---|
| Goodbye | Ordinary |
| Common | Pretty |
| Beautifull | So long. |
| Kind | False |
| Wrong | Gentle |
| Silly | Well |
| Fine | Foolish |
| Young | High |
| Tall | New |

**27.** Complete as frases com **o past tense** dos verbos irregulares do boxe abaixo. Consulte também a tabela de verbos irregulares no final deste caderno.

began – had – went – came – made – left – drank – ate – was – read – learnt

a) I _____ home early yesterday.

b) She _____ her bed before she _____.

c) The boy _____ all the cake!

d) I _____ all thsese books.

e) I _____ to read when I was seven.

f) I _____ thirsty and I _____ two glasses of water.

g) They all _____ away and left me alone.

h) The meeting _____ at 9h10 p.m.

i) I _____ to bed early, because I had to get up at six o'clock.

# Dictation

**28.** Ouça com atenção o ditado que o professor vai apresentar e escreva.

**ANOTAÇÕES**

# Lesson 1 – Irregular verbs

**THE HISTORY OF AMERICA**

In 1620, the Puritans, a religious group, **left** England and **went** to the United States.

They **settled** on the East Coast of the United States.

The Indians **taught** them how to plant. After the first harvest they **held** a feast to thank God.

It **was** the first Thanksgiving Day.

### SOME IRREGULAR VERBS

| Infinitive | Past tense | Past participle |
|---|---|---|
| to become (tornar-se) | became | become |
| to break (quebrar) | broke | broken |
| to begin (começar) | began | begun |
| to bring (trazer) | brought | brought |
| to buy (comprar) | bought | bought |
| to build (construir) | built | built |
| to catch (pegar) | caught | caught |
| to choose (escolher) | chose | chosen |
| to come (vir) | came | come |
| to cost (custar) | cost | cost |
| to cut (cortar) | cut | cut |
| to draw (desenhar) | drew | drawn |
| to drink (beber) | drank | drunk |
| to drive (dirigir) | drove | driven |
| to eat (comer) | ate | eaten |
| to find (encontrar) | found | found |
| to give (dar) | gave | given |
| to go (ir) | went | gone |
| to know (conhecer) | knew | known |
| to hold (realizar) | held | held |
| to teach (ensinar) | taught | taught |

**1.** Traduza o texto da página anterior.

**2.** Responda de acordo com o texto.

a) When did the Puritans leave England?

b) The Puritans left England and went to
( ) India.
( ) the United States.
( ) Brazil.

c) Where did the Puritans settle in the United States?

d) Who taught the Puritans how to plant?

e) What did the Puritans and the Indians do after the first harvest?

**3.** Faça perguntas, empregando a palavra **when** (quando). Observe o exemplo.

The film begins at 7.
**When does the film begin?**

a) She comes to Brazil in May.

b) I go to school in February.

c) The bus leaves at 4 o'clock.

d) They study English at night.

e) The baker gets up early in the morning.

**4.** Continue fazendo perguntas empregando **when** (quando) no tempo passado. Observe o exemplo

The Puritans **left** England in 1620.
**When did the Puritans leave England?**

a) My team **became** champion two years ago.

b) He **became** president last year.

c) She **ate** her last meal yesterday night.

d) I **went** to England in 1998.

e) I **knew** her last year.

f) The company **built** my house 10 years ago.

**5.** Faça perguntas com **what** (o que) no tempo presente. Observe o exemplo.

She always **buys** fruit at the fair.
**What does she always buy at the fair?**

a) Lucy always **buys** vegetables at the fair.

b) They always **drink** water in the morning.

c) The children **build** sandcastles.

d) I always **eat** rice and beans at the restaurant.

e) He always **brings** flowers to his wife.

f) You **give** presents on Christmas.

**6.** Use a palavra **what** para fazer perguntas no tempo passado. Observe o exemplo.

John **broke** his leg in the accident.
**What did John break in the accident?**

a) She brought a present to me.

b) My father caught a big fish.

c) The little girl **cut** her finger.

d) The children **drew** little houses.

e) They **drank** water.

f) We **ate** a delicious sandwich.

g) She **found** a treasure.

h) I **gave** her a watch.

i) Mr Brown **taught** English.

j) The child **held** a red ball in his hands.

**7.** Preencha a cruzadinha com o **past tense** (passado) dos verbos abaixo.

1. to bring (trazer)
2. to draw (desenhar)
3. to begin (começar)
4. to give (dar)
5. to catch (pegar)
6. to know (conhecer)
7. to come (vir)
8. to buy (comprar)
9. to find (encontrar)
10. to go (ir)
11. to eat (comer)
12. to drink (beber)

**8.** Passe as frases para a forma interrogativa. Observe os exemplos.

The film **begins** at 7.
**Does the film begin at 7?**

The film **began** at 7.
**Did the film begin at 7?**

a) Your mother **buys** fruit at the fair.

b) Your mother **bought** vegetables at the fair.

c) They **come** from Brazil.

d) They **came** from Brazil.

e) You **know** my name.

f) You **knew** my name.

g) They **choose** the best fruit.

h) They **chose** the best fruit.

i) They **found** the lesson difficult.

j) They **drank** a lot of water.

k) Your father **drives** his car with attention.

l) The boys **broke** the window with a ball.

m) The goalkeeper **caught** the ball.

n) They **ate** at seven.

o) They **go** to the beach.

p) They **went** to the beach.

**9.** Passe as frases para a forma negativa. Observe os exemplos.

The film **begins** at 7.
The film **does not begin** at 7.
(The film **doesn't begin** at 7.)

The film **began** at 7.
The film **did not begin** at 7.
(The film **didn't begin** at 7.)

a) She **finds** the lesson easy.

b) She **found** the lesson easy.

c) The shirt **costs** ten dollars.

d) The shirt **cost** ten dollars.

e) I **know** your name.

f) She **goes** to school in the morning.

g) They **went** to the club.

h) We **come** from England.

i) My parents **came** from Canada.

j) John **broke** his watch.

k) My brother **builds** houses.

l) He **draws** a landscape.

m) Mary **found** her watch.

n) They **bought** a new car.

**10.** A mensagem rasgada.
(The torn message.)
Descubra a mensagem e escreva-a na linha abaixo.

Th | G | ank
od | f | ever
or | ything

## Dictation

**11.** Ouça com atenção o ditado que o professor vai apresentar e escreva.

**ANOTAÇÕES**

# Lesson 2 – How many books did you buy?

**HOW MANY BOOKS DID YOU BUY?**

– How many story books did you buy?
– I bought four interesting books.
– How much did you spend for them?
– I didn't spend much money.
– How much then?
– Twenty dollars.
– Where did you buy the books?
– In a bookstore near the church.

**1.** Traduza o diálogo acima.

**2.** Responda às perguntas, usando as expressões entre parênteses. Consulte a lista de verbos irregulares no final do livro. Observe o exemplo.
**Lembrete**: Usa-se **much** para coisas não contáveis: water, sugar, milk...

– How much did you pay for this shirt? (ten dollars)
– **I paid ten dollars.**

a) – How much did your notebook cost? (five dollars – to cost – cost – cost: custar)

b) – How much water did you drink?
(two glasses of water – to drink – drank – drunk: beber)

c) – How much sugar did you sell?
(ten packets of sugar – to sell – sold – sold: vender)

d) – How much milk did you buy?
(five bottles of milk – to buy – bought – bought: comprar)

**3.** Responda às perguntas com a expressão **how many** (quantos). Observe o exemplo.

**Lembrete:**

Usa-se o indefinido **many** para seres contáveis: birds, cars...

– How many glasses of milk did she drink?
(five glasses – to drink – drank – drunk: beber)
– She drank five glasses.

a) – How many packets of sugar did you sell?
(ten packets – to sell – sold – sold: vender)

b) – How many dollars did they get?
(five hundred dollars – to get – got – got: conseguir)

c) – How many plates did she break?
(four plates – to break – broke – broken: quebrar)

d) – How many bananas did the monkey eat?
(two bananas – to eat – ate – eaten: comer)

**4.** Preencha as lacunas com verbos no tempo passado (**past tense**).

a) (to find) Sue _____ her documents.

b) (to go) Grace _____ to school in the morning.

c) (to give) I _____ her a nice present in her birthday.

d) (to buy) My parents _____ a very comfortable car.

e) (to begin) The film _____ at 8 o'clock.

f) (to catch) The goalkeeper _____ the ball.

g) (to get up) Nancy _____ an hour ago.

h) (to see) I _____ her at school.

i) (to drive) Sue _____ her car with attention.

**5.** Relacione as frases, de acordo com a tradução.

a) Barbara came from England.
b) Barbara comes from England.
c) He goes by bus to the club.
d) He went by bus to the club.
e) Who knew my name?
f) Who knows my name?
g) I drank a lot of water.
h) I didn't drink much water.
i) I drink a lot of water.
j) The shirt cost 10 dollars.
k) The shirt costs 10 dollars.

( ) Ele foi de ônibus para o clube.
( ) Eu bebi muita água.
( ) Eu não bebi muita água.
( ) Bárbara veio da Inglaterra.
( ) Bárbara vem da Inglaterra.
( ) Ele vai de ônibus para o clube.
( ) A camisa custa 10 dólares.
( ) A camisa custou 10 dólares.
( ) Quem sabia meu nome?
( ) Quem sabe meu nome?
( ) Eu bebo muita água.

**6.** Faça perguntas usando a palavra **where** (onde). Consulte a lista de verbos irregulares no final do livro. Observe o exemplo.

– **Where did the old man fall?**
– The old man **fell** in the street.

a) _____
– I **forgot** my cell telephone at school.

b) _____
– She got new magazines at the airport.

c)
   – They went to the beach.

d)                    ?
   – I heard that story at school.

e)
   – The dangerous thief hid behind a bush fence.

f)
   – I hurt my leg in the football game.

g)
   – Jane **kept** her clothes in the wardrobe.

h)
   – I **learnt** (learned) English at school.

i)
   – I **left** my bag under the desk.

j)
   – She **put** her pen in the purse.

k)
   – People **ran** to the supermarket yesterday.

l)
   – A thief **stole** candies in the supermarket.

m)
   – Women **wore** long dresses at the marriage party.

n)
   – My team **won** the last game in Rio.

**7.** Ligue as perguntas às respectivas respostas.

a) – Did you feel cold yesterday night?
b) – What time does the bus leave?
c) – Do you speak English?
d) – Were you at Jane's party yesterday?
e) – Where did she buy fruit?
f) – Who sells newspapers nearby?
g) – Did you drink water yesterday?

( ) – At a greengrocer's on Colorado Street.
( ) – No, I don't.
( ) – The newsagent on Carolina Street.
( ) – No, I didn't, but I drank a lot

of fruit juice.

( ) – Yes, I did. I forgot my blouse at home.

( ) – At six o'clock in the morning.

( ) – No, I wasn't.

**FUN TIME**
- My brother fell from a twenty-five meter tree this morning.
- Did he hurt himself very much?
- No, he had climbed up only one meter.

How do you spell the name of the capital of the United States: Nova Iorque or New York?

She **ran** in the park.
**Did she run in the park?**

a) The plants **grow** fast.

b) The plants **grew** fast.

c) The bus **leaves** at 6.

d) The bus **left** at 6.

e) He **keeps** his money in a bank.

f) He **kept** his money in a bank.

g) John **shuts** the shop at noon.

**9.** Passe as frases para a forma negativa. Observe os exemplos.

She **runs** in the park.
**She does not run in the park.**

**8.** Passe as frases para a forma interrogativa. Observe os exemplos.

She runs in the park.
**Does she run in the park?**

She **ran** in the park.
She **did not run** in the park.

a) The plants **grow** fast.

b) The plants **grew** fast.

c) The bus **leaves** at 6.

d) The bus **left** at 6.

e) He **keeps** his money in a bank.

f) He **kept** his money in a bank.

g) John **shuts** the shop at noon.

h) John **shut** the shop at noon.

**10.** Preencha a cruzadinha em inglês.

**Across** (horizontal)
1. Número 1.
5. Número 8.
6. Pronome possessivo neutro usado para coisas e animais.

**Down** (vertical)
2. Noite.
3. Número 10.
4. Uma das formas verbais:
    eat – ate – eaten (comer – comeu – comido)

**11.** Jogo dos verbos irregulares. Os alunos, dois a dois, jogam o dado alternadamente. De acordo com a casa sorteada, o aluno deverá responder à pergunta. Caso não saiba responder, volta à posição **START**.
Vence quem chegar primeiro à posição **FINISH**.

Perguntas de 1 a 5: falar o tempo passado dos verbos (**past tense**)
de 6 a 10: falar as frases no tempo passado (**past tense**)
de 11 a 15: falar as frases na forma interrogativa
de 16 a 20: falar as frases na forma negativa

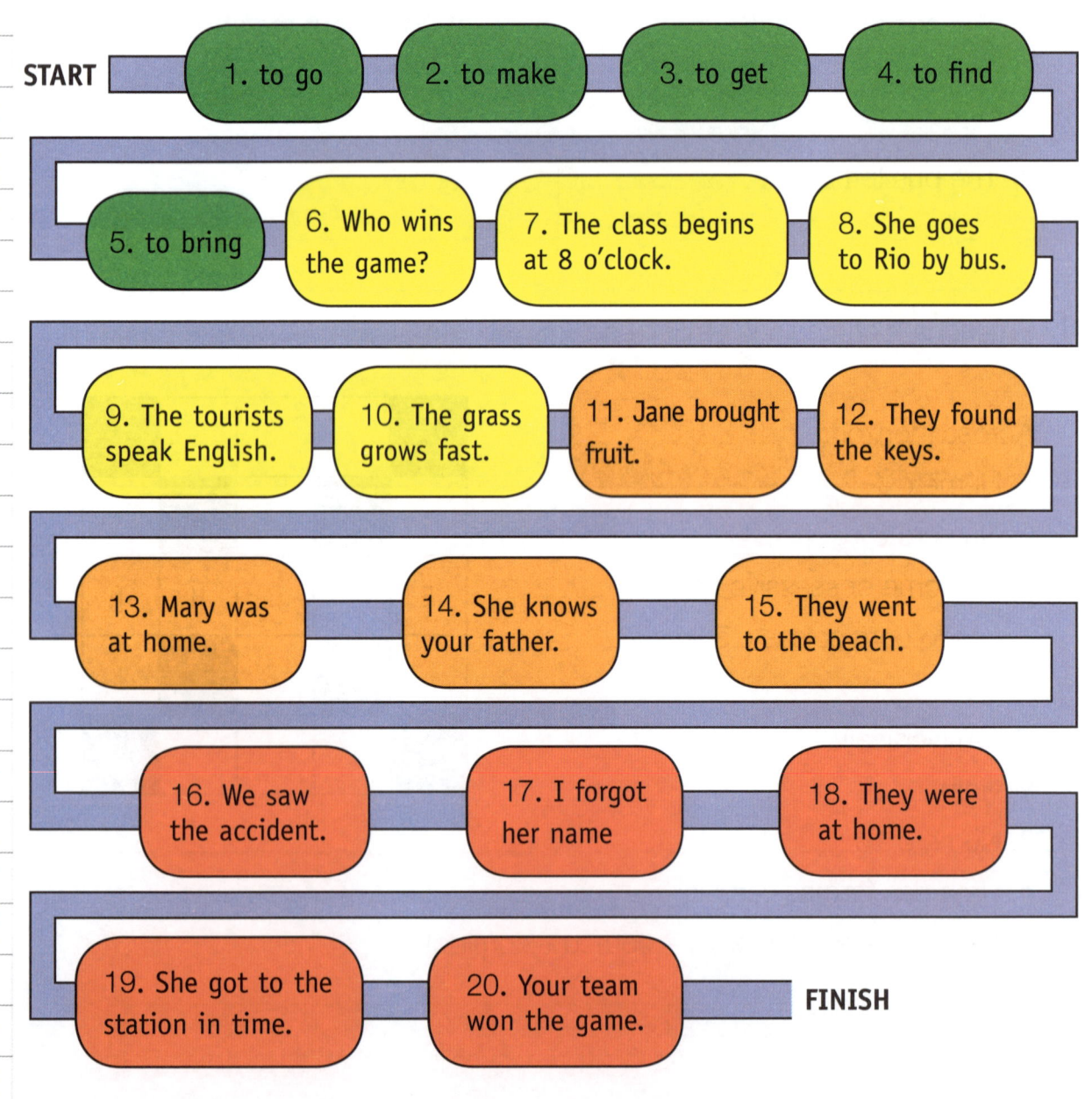

START

1. to go
2. to make
3. to get
4. to find
5. to bring
6. Who wins the game?
7. The class begins at 8 o'clock.
8. She goes to Rio by bus.
9. The tourists speak English.
10. The grass grows fast.
11. Jane brought fruit.
12. They found the keys.
13. Mary was at home.
14. She knows your father.
15. They went to the beach.
16. We saw the accident.
17. I forgot her name
18. They were at home.
19. She got to the station in time.
20. Your team won the game.

FINISH

## Dictation

**12.** Ouça com atenção o ditado que o professor vai apresentar e escreva.

**13.** Complete as frases com o **past tense** dos verbos irregulares do quadro abaixo.

> came – left – knew – read – ate – went – began – was – learned – made – had – drank

a) I _____ home early yesterday.

b) She _____ her bed before she _____.

c) The boy _____ all the cake!

d) I _____ all these books.

e) I _____ to read when I was seven.

f) I _____ thirsty, so I _____ two glasses of water.

g) They all _____ away and _____ me alone.

h) The meeting _____ at 9h10 p.m.

i) I _____ to bed early, because

j) I _____ to get up at six o'clock.

**14.** Complete com "**how many**" ou "**how much**".

a) _____ bananas do you eat in a week?

b) _____ money did you get last mounth?

c) _____ water is there in the glass?

d) _____ apples are there in the basket?

e) _____ time do you spend to go to school?

f) _____ people were there in the stadium?

g) _____ states are there in Brazil?

h) _____ water do you drink a day?

i) _____ stars are there in the Brazilian flag?

# Lesson 3 – I have some friends

### PRONOMES INDEFINIDOS

1) **Any** e seus compostos em frases afirmativas têm sentido de qualquer, quaisquer, nenhum.

Take **any** candy you want.
(Pegue qualquer doce que você quiser.)

**Anyone** can solve the problem.
(Qualquer um pode resolver o problema.)

Choose **anything**.
(Escolha qualquer coisa.)

Is there **anybody** here?
(Há alguém aqui?)

2) Usam-se **some**, **something**, **somebody** e **someone** em pergunta, quando se espera uma resposta afirmativa.
Isso acontece, por exemplo, quando se oferece comida ou bebida:

Do you like **some** juice?
Would you like **some** juice?
(Você gostaria de tomar um pouco de suco?)

Do you have any friends in England?

No, I don't have any friends in England, but I have some friends in Brazil.

Muitas vezes **some** e **any** dispensam tradução.
Equivalem em português a um pouco de, algum, nenhum. Observe:

I need **some** money.
(Eu preciso de dinheiro. Eu preciso de algum dinheiro. Eu preciso de um pouco de dinheiro.)
There is not **any** milk in the fridge.
(Não há leite na geladeira. Não há nenhum leite na geladeira.)

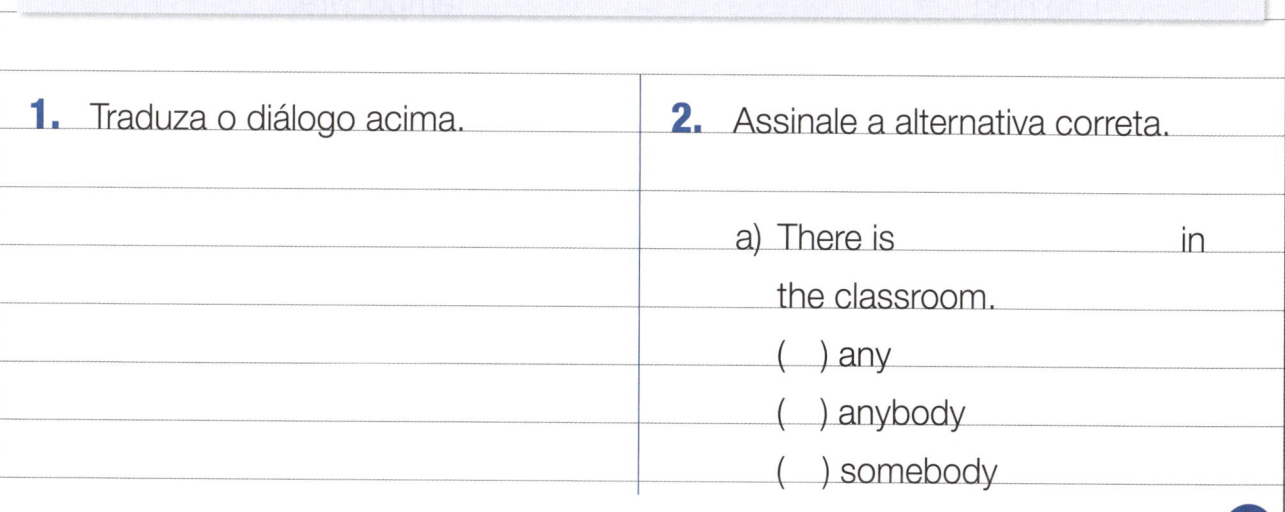

---

**1.** Traduza o diálogo acima.

**2.** Assinale a alternativa correta.

a) There is _____ in the classroom.
( ) any
( ) anybody
( ) somebody

b) What are you doing?
( ) any
( ) nothing
( ) some

c) What do you want?
( ) some eggs
( ) any
( ) none

d) I don't have _____ sugar.
( ) some
( ) any
( ) nothing

e) They bought _____ vegetables at the fair.
( ) some
( ) any
( ) no one

f) Do you have _____ doubts?
( ) nothing
( ) not
( ) any

**3.** Traduza as frases.

a) Would you like something to drink?

b) I bought nothing.
   I didn't buy anything.

**4.** Complete as frases com **some** ou **any** e ligue às suas respectivas traduções.

a) Do you have _____ doubt?
b) Would you like _____ tea?
c) I don't need _____ help.
d) Do you need _____ money?
e) I can see _____ stars in the sky.
f) I don't have _____ free time.
g) She can't go with you. She has _____ problems to solve.
h) There were _____ rotten pears in the box.

( ) Eu não tenho nenhum tempo livre.
( ) Você precisa de (algum) dinheiro?
( ) Havia algumas peras podres na caixa.
( ) Você tem alguma dúvida?
( ) Você gostaria de um pouco de chá?
( ) Ela não pode ir com você.

Ela tem alguns problemas para resolver.
( ) Eu não preciso de (nenhuma) ajuda.
( ) Eu posso ver algumas estrelas no céu.

**5.** Complete as frases com os indefinidos **some, any, somebody** ou **someone, anybody** ou **anyone, nobody, something, anything**.

a) We don't have _____ fruit at home; please bring _____ from the supermarket.
b) I didn't see _____ good movies last month.
c) Is there _____ at the door?
 No, there is _____.
d) These problems are very easy. _____ can solve them.
e) Do you have _____ experience as a waiter?
f) There isn't _____ money in my purse.
g) I am hungry. Do you have _____ to eat?
h) I need _____ fruit to make fruit juice.
i) Do you have _____ money, Julie?
 Yes, I have _____.
 And you, Grace?
 I don't have _____.

**6.** Observe as formas que a língua inglesa possui para expressar a mesma ideia.

There is **nothing** to do.
There **isn't anything** to do.
(Não há nada para fazer.)

I have **no** money.
**I don't have any money**.
(Eu não tenho nenhum dinheiro.)

Baseado nos exemplos acima, continue o exercício, empregando a outra forma negativa.

a) There is nothing in the box.

b) I have no time.

c) There is nobody in the toilet.

d) I have no friends.

e) I didn't catch any fish.

**7.** Dê respostas negativas. Observe os exemplos.

– Is there anybody in the room?
– **No, there is nobody.**
– **There is not anybody.**
– Did anybody see the accident?
– **No, nobody saw the accident.**

a) – Did Nancy get any money?

b) – Did you invite anybody to your birthday?

c) – Did anybody here find my keys?

**8.** Preencha as lacunas com **some** ou **any**.

a) I would like _____ coffee.
b) She doesn't have _____ money.
c) Jane has _____ pretty blouses.
d) The poor family received _____ food.
e) There aren't _____ eggs in the basket.
f) There is not _____ money in my purse.
g) Do you have _____ suggestion?
h) Would you like _____ water?
i) _____ girls are very kind.
j) You are not well. You should take _____ medicine.
k) Do you see _____ cats on the roof?
l) No, I can't see _____ because it is dark.
m) Mary borrowed _____ money from her friend.
n) I don't have _____ time to play with you.
o) I have _____ ideas about the origin of the universe.

**9.** Escreva **A** diante dos indefinidos usados em frases afirmativas e **IN** diante dos indefinidos usados em frases interrogativas ou negativas.

( ) some
( ) any
( ) somebody
( ) anybody
( ) someone
( ) something
( ) anything
( ) anyone

**10.** Complete as frases com **somebody, something, anybody, anything.**

a) I know _____ who can help you.
b) I have _____ important to tell you.
c) Did I say _____ wrong?
d) Did you find _____ in the purse?
e) Is there _____ in the box?
f) I can't help _____ now.
g) Is there _____ at home?
h) There isn't _____ studying in the room.
i) I am hungry. Is there _____ to eat?

**11.** Passe as frases para a forma negativa. Observe o exemplo.

There are **some** pencils in the box.
There are not any pencils in the box.
There are no pencils in the box.

a) There are **some** birds in the cage.

b) I have **some** money.

c) I have **some** problems.

d) She has **some** friends.

e) Mary bought **some** eggs.

f) There is **something** in the box.

g) There is **something** in the fridge.

h) There is **something** important to declare.

i) There is **somebody** at the door.

j) There is **somebody** calling you.

k) There is **somebody** waiting for you.

**12.** Passe as frases para a forma interrogativa. Observe o exemplo.

There are **some** pencils in the box.
**Are there any pencils in the box?**

a) There are **some** birds in the cage.

b) She found **some** money.

c) Nancy bought **some** eggs.

d) There is **somebody** in the house.

e) There is **something** in the box.

f) You have **some** problems.

g) Mary invited **somebody** to the party.

h) There is **somebody** calling you.

i) There is **something** to eat on the table.

**13.** Complete com palavras à sua escolha, em inglês.

a) The world I imagine has truth, happiness,

b) The world I imagine has no poverty, no corruption,

**14.** Traduza os provérbios:
No bees, no honey.
No work, no money.

**15.** Observe o exemplo e escreva os diálogos.

salad/tomatoes

– What are you going to make?
– I am going to make a delicious salad. I need **some** tomatoes. Do you have **any** tomatoes?
– Sorry. I have **no** tomatoes.

bread/wheat flour

cake/eggs

barbecue/salt

# Lesson 4 – I don't have much money

**Paulo:** Wow Teacher! there are so **many** books in this library!

**Teacher:** Yes, Paul.

**Paulo:** I don't have **much** money to buy books. Can I take this one to read in my house?

**Teacher:** Sure! Reading is very important to develop your mind.

## MUCH – LITTLE / MANY – FEW

**Much:** muito
**Little:** pouco

Usamos **much** e **little** para coisas que não podemos contar por unidades, como água, leite, café, farinha, tempo, comida, trabalho, barulho etc.

**Much** water. (Muita água.)
**Little** milk. (Pouco leite.)
**Much** coffee. (Muito café.)
**Little** flour. (Pouca farinha.)
**Much** time. (Muito tempo.)
**Much** food. (Muita comida.)

**Many** (a lot of): muitos
**Few:** poucos

Usamos **many** e **few** para coisas contáveis, como pássaros, livros, carros, rapazes etc.

**Many** birds (**a lot of** birds): muitos pássaros.
**Few** books. (Poucos livros.)
**Many** cars. (Muitos carros.)
**Few** boys. (Poucos meninos.)

**1.** Traduza o diálogo acima.

**MONEY FOR MEG'S LUNCH**

– Meg, come back here. Do you have some money for your lunch?
– Mom, I don't have **much** money. Just **a few** dollars... one, two dollars.
– Take forty dollars.
– Mom, I don't need **many** dollars. Five dollars is enough.

**2.** Traduza o diálogo acima.

**3.** Complete as frases com **there is** ou **there are/much/little/many/few/a lot of/so many**. Observe o exemplo.

**There are many** unemployed people in Brazil.

a) _____ people in China. (1.300.000.000) (About one billion and three hundred million people)

b) _____ water in the Northeast of Brazil.

c) _____ birds and wild animals in the Amazon forest.

d) _____ rich people in Brazil.

e) _____ poor people in Brazil.

f) _____ not violence in small towns of Brazil.

g) _____ food for _____ families in the Northeast of Brazil.

h) _____ poor students reach the university in Brazil.

> **Observação:**
> Geralmente não se usa **much** em frases afirmativas e interrogativas. Neste caso use: **a lot of**, **lots of** ou **a great deal of** = muito, uma porção de, uma grande quantidade de...

**4.** Passe para a forma negativa as frases a seguir. Use o indefinido **much**. Observe o exemplo.

I spent **a lot of** time at the restaurant.
I didn't spend much time at the restaurant.

a) She drinks **a great deal** of water during the day.

b) George puts **a lot of** salt on his salad.

c) Jane has **a lot of** money in the bank.

d) She has **a lot of** patience with children.

e) They have **a lot of** love to give.

f) The baker used **a lot of** flour yesterday.

g) The maid uses **a lot of** soap to wash our clothes.

**5.** Escreva o contrário, mudando **many** ou **a lot of** por **few**.

a) We entered **a lot of** shops.

b) I have **many** friends.

c) There are **a lot of** cars in the streets.

d) There are **many** girls in the club.

e) I know **a lot of** people in my school.

f) There were **few** books on the table.

## Dictation

**6.** Ouça com atenção o ditado que o professor vai apresentar e escreva.

ANOTAÇÕES

# Lesson 5 – Comparative degree

Ted is **shorter than** his brother Tony.
Tony is **older than** his brother Ted.

COMPARATIVO DE SUPERIORIDADE

**Short adjectives:** Formamos o comparativo de superioridade dos adjetivos curtos (formados por uma ou duas sílabas) acrescentando, geralmente, **-er** ao final deles e a palavra **than** (do que), exemplo:

I am fast**er than** you.
(Sou mais rápido do que você).

**Long adjectives:** Os adjetivos longos ficam invariáveis no grau comparativo. Com estes adjetivos o grau comparativo segue o modelo:

**more + adjective + than**

Jane is **more beautiful than** Meg.
(Jane é mais bonita do que Meg.)

1) Os adjetivos de uma sílaba, formados por consoante(s) + vogal + consoante, dobram a última consoante, exemplo:
**big** – bi**gger than** (maior do que);
**thin** – thi**nner than** (mais magro do que).

2) Com os adjetivos de duas sílabas terminados por **ous**, **ish**, **ful**, **ed**, **nt**, **ing**, usamos **more** no comparativo e **the most** no superlativo, exemplo:
**more** famous (comparativo);
**the most** famous (superlativo).

3) Os **short adjectives** terminados em **y** precedido de consoante trocam o **y** por **i**, acrescentando **-er** no final, exemplo:
**happy** – happ**ier than** (mais feliz do que);
**crazy** – craz**ier than** (mais doido do que).

4) **Irregular comparatives:** alguns adjetivos formam o comparativo de superioridade de forma irregular.
**good** – **better than** (melhor do que);
**bad** – **worse than** (pior do que).

Observe o exemplo:
Your bicycle is **better than** mine.
(Sua bicicleta é melhor do que a minha.)

COMPARATIVO DE IGUALDADE

Se quisermos expressar igualdade entre dois seres ou coisas, usamos a forma

**as + adjective + as**
She is **as pretty as** her sister.

COMPARATIVO DE INFERIORIDADE

Se quisermos expressar inferioridade de um ser ou coisa com relação a outro, há duas maneiras de expressar:

**less... than** = Marc is **less** tall **than** Dida.
e
**not so... as** = Marc is **not so** tall **as** Dida.

**1.** Observe a fotografia com os dois irmãos e responda.

a) Who is tall in the picture?
   **Ted is.**

b) Who is short?

c) Who is thin in the picture?

d) Who is fat?

e) Is Ted taller than Tony?

f) Is Tony taller than Ted?

g) Is Ted fatter than Tony?

h) Is Tony fatter than Ted?

**2.** Observe o exemplo e redija os diálogos.

ferocious
the lion — the wolf

a) – Which animal is more ferocious: the lion or the wolf?
   – The lion is **more** ferocious **than** the wolf.

beautiful
the daisy — the rose

b)

comfortable
the hut — the mansion

c)

expensive

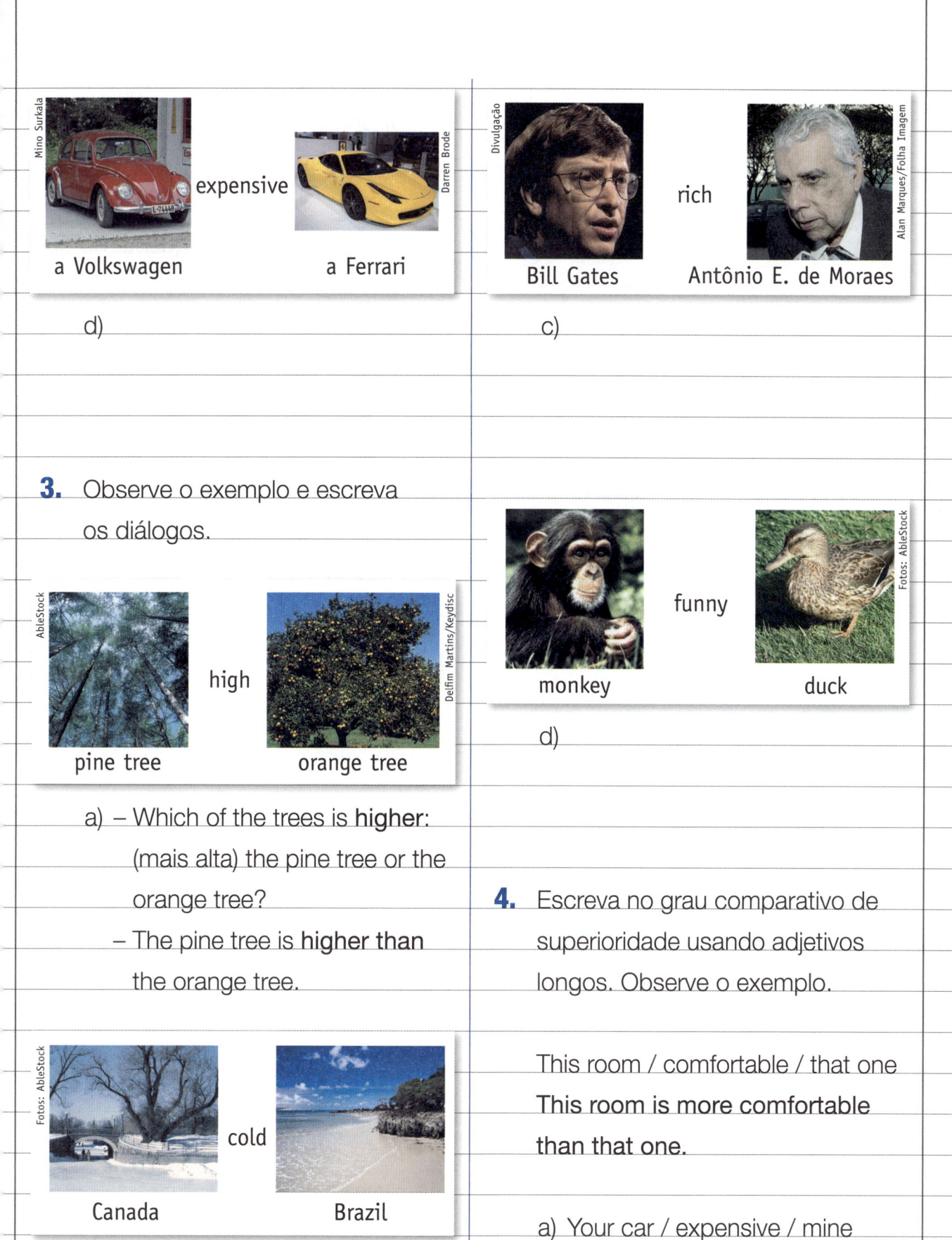

a Volkswagen     a Ferrari

d)

rich

Bill Gates     Antônio E. de Moraes

c)

**3.** Observe o exemplo e escreva os diálogos.

high

pine tree     orange tree

funny

monkey     duck

d)

a) – Which of the trees is **higher**: (mais alta) the pine tree or the orange tree?
– The pine tree is **higher than** the orange tree.

**4.** Escreva no grau comparativo de superioridade usando adjetivos longos. Observe o exemplo.

This room / comfortable / that one
**This room is more comfortable than that one.**

cold

Canada     Brazil

a) Your car / expensive / mine

b)

51

b) Japanese / difficult / Portuguese

c) These stories / interesting / those ones

d) A butterfly / beautiful / a fly

**5.** Escreva no grau comparativo, em inglês. Observe o exemplo.

São Paulo é maior do que Belém. (big / bigger)
**São Paulo is bigger than Belém.**

a) Esta lição é mais fácil do que aquela. (easy / easier)

b) Sua casa é mais antiga do que a minha. (antique)

c) Este exercício é mais difícil do que aquele. (difficult)

d) James é mais alto do que Peter. (tall / taller)

e) O café está mais quente do que o leite. (hot / hotter)

f) O Brasil é mais populoso do que a Argentina. (populous)

**6.** Relacione os antônimos.

( a ) better
( b ) taller
( c ) bigger
( d ) richer
( e ) happier

(   ) worse
(   ) sadder
(   ) smaller
(   ) poorer
(   ) shorter

> **Lembre que:**
>
> O comparativo **as... as** expressa igualdade entre dois seres ou coisas.
>
> Os comparativos **less... than** e **not so... as** expressam posição de inferioridade entre dois seres ou coisas.

**7.** Escreva as frases no comparativo de igualdade ou de inferioridade. Observe o exemplo.

Paul / kind / Mary (as...as)
**Paul is as kind as Mary.**

a) Paul / young / Beth (less...than)

b) Susan / pretty / Lisa (not so...as)

c) French team / good / Brazilian team (not so...as)

d) The cat / fast / the rabbit (as...as)

e) Your city / noisy / mine (not so...as)

f) You / intelligent / me (as...as)

**ANOTAÇÕES**

# Review – Lessons 1, 2, 3, 4 and 5

**1.** Mude as frases afirmativas para a forma interrogativa.

a) They are sitting at the round table.

b) You are satisfied.

c) They like coffee.

d) She loves you.

e) They invited the social assistant.

f) You lost the key.

g) The class began at 7.

h) You sold the old car.

i) They understood the lesson.

**2.** Mude as frases afirmativas para a forma negativa.

a) This food is good.

b) She was at home a week ago.

c) They get a lot of money.

d) She played the piano.

e) The secretary wrote the letter.

f) She lost the key.

g) They told the truth.

h) The cat drank the milk.

**3.** Traduza para o inglês.

a) Eu não tenho nenhum dinheiro.

b) Há alguém na porta?
   Não, não há ninguém.

c) Você comprou alguma coisa no supermercado?

**4.** Complete com **some** ou **any**.

a) I have _____ friends in Rio.

b) I don't have _____ money.

c) We made _____ suggestions.

d) The teacher explained _____ problems.

e) I'm learning _____ new words in English.

f) There are _____ people waiting for you.

g) Did you have _____ friends in the United States?

h) The pupils didn't ask _____ questions.

i) There wasn't _____ news.

**5.** Complete com **somebody**, **something**, **anybody**, **anything**.

a) Helen didn't invite _____ to her birthday party.

b) I want to buy _____ for my friend.

c) Did _____ knock at the door?

d) Is there _____ in the box?

e) No, there isn't _____ in the box.

f) Did you see _____ talking in the class?

g) No, I didn't see _____ talking in the class.

h) Is there _____ interesting in this paper?

i) No, there isn't _____ interesting in this paper.

**6.** Responda usando **nobody** ou **nothing**. Observe o exemplo.

– Is there anybody in the room?
– No, there is **nobody**.

a) – Is there anything in the box?

b) – Did you buy anything in the supermarket?

c) – Is there anything I can do for you?

d) – Did anybody call me?

e) – Did she give anything to you?

**7.** Responda às perguntas na forma afirmativa e negativa. Observe o exemplo.

– Have you got **any** coffee?
– Yes, I have **some**.
– No, I haven't got **any**.

a) – Have you got any sugar?

b) – Have you got any butter?

c) – Have you got any money?

d) – Has she got any work to do?

e) – Have you got any pencils?

**8.** Escreva os adjetivos no comparativo de superioridade.

new:
slow:
small:
big:
hot:
easy:

**9.** Observe a figura e o exemplo e compare os dois carros.

a) small
b) comfortable
c) beautiful
d) slow
e) cheap
f) expensive
g) dirty
h) economical
i) big
j) fast

a) The new car is smaller than the old car.

b)

c)

d)

e)

f)

g)

h)

i)

j)

**10.** Use **as...as** no comparativo de igualdade. Observe o exemplo.

Mary – beautiful – Jane
**Mary is as beautiful as Jane.**

a) John – funny – Paul

b) Today – hot – yesterday

c) This lesson – easy – the last one

d) This lesson – easy – the last one

e) Gordon – tall – Jim

f) Japanese – difficult – English

**ANOTAÇÕES**

**11.** Observe o exemplo e forme frases com o comparativo de superioridade.

I – old – you
**I am older than you.**

a) Mary – beautiful – Jane

b) Carol – young – you

c) Today – cold – yesterday

# Lesson 6 – Superlative

**Look at these pictures:**

I'm the tallest!

I'm the most ferocious!

And I'm the most intelligent!

I'm the fattest!

I'm the fastest!

### THE SUPERLATIVE

1) Formamos o superlativo dos **short adjectives** (uma ou duas sílabas) seguindo o esquema abaixo, exemplo:

$$\text{The most} + \text{long adjectives} \Rightarrow \begin{cases} \text{in} \\ \text{of} \\ \text{that} \end{cases}$$

Albert is **the** tall**est** boy **in** my class.

a) Ao formar o superlativo, alguns **short adjectives of one syllable** dobram a consoante final (se houver apenas uma vogal), exemplo:

big – **the** b**iggest**: o maior (de todos);
hot – **the** ho**ttest**: o mais quente (de todos).

b) Os **short adjectives** terminados em **y** precedido de consoante trocam o **y** por **i** e acrescentam **est** ao formar o superlativo, exemplo:

ha**ppy** – the happ**iest**: o mais feliz (de todos);
hea**vy** – the heav**iest**: o mais pesado (de todos);
la**zy** – the laz**iest**: o mais preguiçoso (de todos);
fu**nny** – the funn**iest**: o mais engraçado (de todos).

c) **Irregular superlatives**: alguns adjetivos formam o superlativo de maneira irregular.

good – **the best**: o melhor (de todos)
This is **the best** way to get there.
(Este é o melhor caminho para chegar lá.)
bad – **the worst**: o pior (de todos)

2) Formamos o superlativo dos **long adjectives** (duas ou mais sílabas ex.: **beautiful, important, dangerous, comfortable, expensive, etc.**) seguindo o esquema abaixo:

$$\text{The + short adjectives + est} \longleftarrow \begin{cases} \text{in} \\ \text{of} \\ \text{that} \end{cases}$$

Football is **the most popular** sport **in** the world.

**1.** Observe as figuras e responda às perguntas.

a) There are five different animals on the last page. Which of them is the most ferocious?

b) Which of the five animals are not ferocious?

c) Why is the man different from the other animals?

d) Which of them is the fastest?

e) The lion is ferocious. The panther is ferocious too. Is the panther more ferocious than the lion?

f) Is the pig taller or shorter than the giraffe?

g) Which of them is the tallest?

**2.** Relacione corretamente.

1. man's legs
2. internet
3. motorcycle
4. airplane

a) The most dangerous means of transportation. ( )

b) The most primitive means of transportation. ( )

c) The most modern means of transportation. ( )

d) The most modern means of communication. ( )

e) The fastest means of transportation. ( )

f) The slowest means of transportation. ( )

g) The most comfortable means of transportation. ( )

h) The most expensive means of transportation. ( )

**3.** Observe os exemplos e redija os diálogos.

lion     tiger     panther

– All these animals are very ferocious. Which of them is **the most ferocious** animal?
– **The most ferocious** animal is the lion.

deer     tiger     panther

– All these animals are very fast. Which of them is **the fastest** animal?
– **The fastest** animal is the panther.

pig     cow     elephant

a) All these animals are very heavy.

Nancy (49 kg)   Gina (52 kg)   Carol (51 kg)

b) All these models are very thin.

apple cake   nut cake

cream cake   chocolate cake

d) All these cakes are very delicious.

Kate   Lisa
Helen   Sandy

c) All these girls are very beautiful.

Brazil   Mexico   Russia

e) All these countries are very large.

rose  · lily

daisy  · jasmine

f) Here are some fragrant flowers.

**4.** Traduza a canção.

**MY LOVE**
My love is warmer than the warmest sunshine,
Softer than a sigh.
My love is deeper than the deepest ocean,
Wider than the sky.
My love is brighter than the brightest star that shines every night above,
And there is nothing in this world
That can ever change my love.
(From an American Folk-Song)

**ANOTAÇÕES**

## Gabi's Pet Shop (cats and dogs)

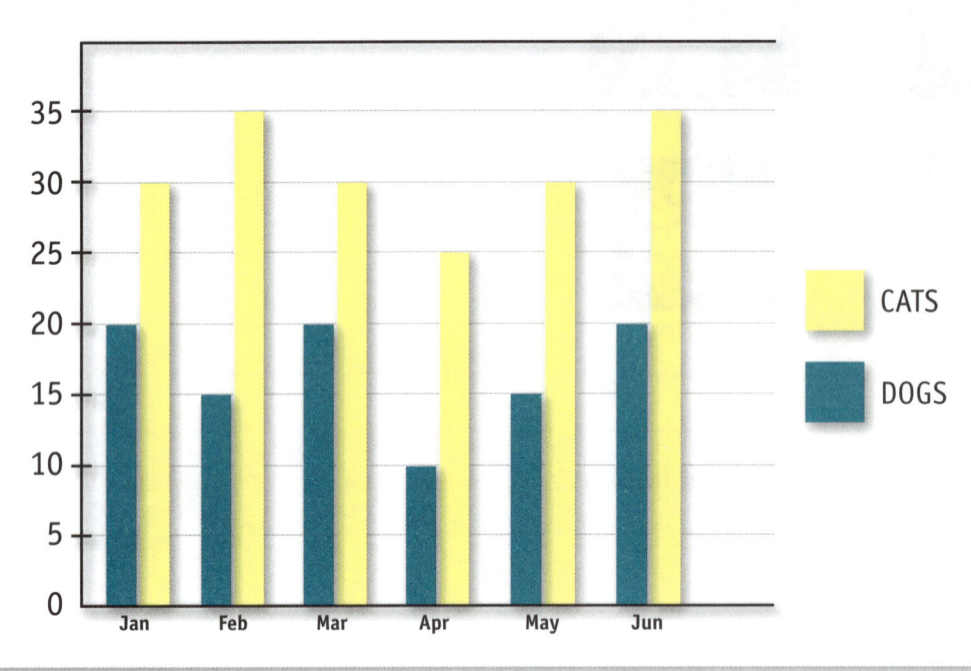

**5.** Observe o gráfico de barras e complete as frases.

This bar graph shows how many _____ and _____ were sold at Gabi's Pet Shop from _____ to _____.

**6.** Observe o gráfico de barras e responda às perguntas.

a) What color bar is used to show cat sales?

b) What was the largest number of cats sold in one month?

c) What was the largest number of dogs sold in one month?

d) Which pet was sold the least in one month?

e) How many dogs were sold from January to June?

f) How many cats were sold in the same period?

Sahara is the world's largest desert area, extending from the Atlantic to the Red Sea, in Northern Africa.

Mount Everest in Nepal is the highest peak in the world. It's 8848 meters high.

## Dictation

**7.** Ouça com atenção o ditado que o professor vai apresentar e escreva.

# Lesson 7 – Present perfect tense

Bruno has visited her grandparents many times.
(Bruno tem visitado seus avós muitas vezes.)

I have worked here since 1990.
(Eu tenho trabalhado aqui desde 1990.)

### PRESENT PERFECT TENSE (PRETÉRITO PERFEITO COMPOSTO)

O **present perfect tense** consiste no emprego do verbo ter no presente do indicativo seguido do particípio passado do verbo principal:

has
       +    past participle
have

O **present perfect tense** deve ser usado nos seguintes casos:

1) Quando relatamos uma ação ocorrida no tempo passado, porém sem que determinemos a data ou o momento em que ela ocorreu ou foi realizada, exemplo:
I **have slept** late.
(Eu tenho dormido tarde.)
Porém, se determinamos a data ou o momento em que a ação se realiza, devemos empregar o **simple past tense**:
I **slept late** yesterday.
(Eu dormi tarde ontem.)

2) Quando nos referimos a uma ação que acabou de ser feita:
My son **has** just **arrived**!
(Meu filho acabou de chegar!)

3) Quando nos referimos a uma ação (ou fato) que se repete várias vezes no passado, sem menção do tempo exato. Veja:
I **have visited** my parents many times.
(Eu tenho visitado meus pais muitas vezes.)

4) Quando nos referimos a uma ação (ou fato) que começou no passado mas que ainda persiste até o momento presente. Observe:
I **have worked** here since 1990.
(Eu tenho trabalhado aqui desde 1990.)

**1.** Preencha a cruzadinha escrevendo o particípio passado dos verbos regulares (que terminam em **ed**) e irregulares (consulte a lista no final do livro.)

1) to live       6) to take
2) to give       7) to buy
3) to spend      8) to write
4) to work       9) to invite
5) to tell       10) to do

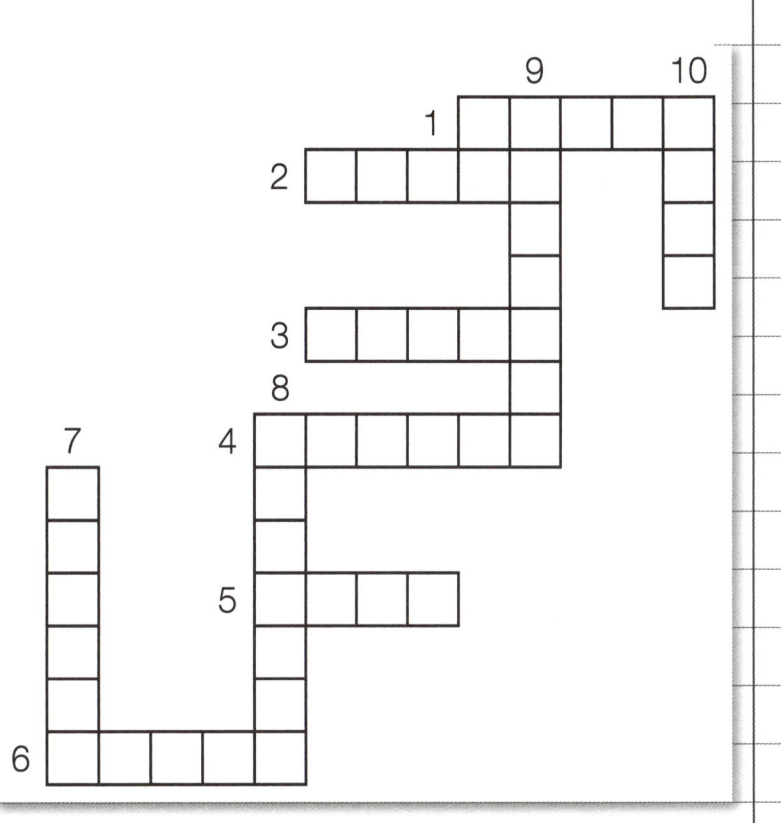

**Observação:**

O **presente perfect tense** frequentemente é acompanhado de alguns advérbios ou preposições, como **just** (exatamente), **since** (desde), **for** (por), **yet** (ainda), **already** (já), **never** (nunca), **ever** (já).

**Helen**: Hello, Jane!
**Jane**: Hi, Helen!
**Helen**: Jane, come to my house! I have just made a delicious cake.
**Jane**: Humm! I'm going there in a few minutes. See you soon!
**Helen**: Bye!

**2.** Traduza o diálogo a acima.

**3.** Aprenda como expressar, em inglês, uma ação que acaba de ser feita (**just**: agora mesmo, há pouco, justamente) Observe os exemplos e monte as frases.

I – finish – the exercises
**I have just finished** the exercises.
**I've just finished** the exercises.
**Eu acabei de concluir** os exercícios.

She – find – the keys
**She has just found** the keys.
**She's just found** the keys.
**Ela acabou de encontrar** as chaves.

a) I – call – her

b) They – discover – the secret

c) I – catch – a fish

d) He – eat – an apple

**4.** Traduza a frase abaixo.

My mother has just arrived from work.

**5.** Complete as frases com o **present perfect** ou com o **simple past**.

a) to win – won – won: ganhar, vencer
My team _____ the game yesterday.
Your team _____ all games lately.

b) to drop – dropped – dropped: derrubar, cair
I _____ any glasses. (negativa)
I _____ two glasses in the kitchen yesterday. (afirmativa)

c) to find – found – found: encontrar
I _____ some coins in the playground.
I _____ some coins in the playground yesterday.

d) to live – lived – lived: morar, viver
They _____ for some time in the United States.
They _____ in the United States last year.

e) to arrive – arrived – arrived: chegar
The bus _____ late yesterday.
The bus _____ late for a week.

f) to be – was/were – been: ser, estar
It _____ hot since December.
It _____ cold yesterday night.

g) to tell – told – told: contar, dizer
Some politicians _____ many lies last year.
Some politicians _____ many lies.

h) to see – saw – seen: ver
_____ you _____ my friend Nancy?
Yes, I _____ her at the snack bar yesterday morning.

**6.** Observe o uso do **since** (desde), **for** (por, durante) e **yet** (ainda) com o **present perfect tense** e depois complete as frases com essas palavras. Observe os exemplos.

She **has been** sick **since** Monday. (Ela tem estado doente desde segunda-feira.)

She **has been** sick **for** a long time. (Ela tem estado doente por um longo tempo.)

She **hasn't left** the hospital **yet**. (Ela não deixou o hospital ainda.)

a) I **haven't seen** that film _____.

b) They **have played** in our team _____ 1985.

c) Ronaldinho **has played** football in Spain _____ a long period.

d) **Haven't** you **seen** that film _____ ?

e) They **haven't eaten** _____ .

f) Diana **hasn't bought** the tickets _____ .

g) She **has been** sleeping _____ ten hours.

h) Joe **has lived** in California since 1998.

i) My father **has been** a taxi driver _____ years and years.

**7.** Observe o emprego dos advérbios **ever** (já) e **never** (nunca) com o present perfect tense.

to be – was – **been** (ser, estar)
– Have you **ever** been to England? (Você já foi à Inglaterra?)
– No, I have **never** been to England. (Não, eu nunca estive na Inglaterra.)

to eat – ate – **eaten** (comer)
– Have you **ever** eaten octopus?
– No, I've **never** eaten octopus.

a) to drink – drank – **drunk** (beber)
– Have you **ever** drunk coffee?

b) to kiss – kissed – **kissed** (beijar)
– Have you **ever** kissed her?

c) to see – saw – **seen** (ver)
– Has she **ever** seen the sea?

**8.** Observe os exemplos. A seguir, escreva os verbos no futuro imediato, no tempo presente contínuo e no pretérito perfeito composto.

**Immediate future**

Mary / to cross the street.
**Mary is going to cross the street.**
(Mary vai atravessar a rua.)

**Present continuous tense**

**She is crossing the street.**
(Ela está atravessando a rua.)

**Present perfect tense**

**She has just crossed the street.**
(Ela acabou de atravessar a rua.)

a) Jane / to eat an orange.

b) Liz / to drink coffee.

c) Nancy / to buy some flowers.

**9.** Complete as lacunas com a forma correta dos verbos em negrito.

a) I **work** here now.
   I have _____ here for a month.

b) I **live** in São Paulo.
   I have _____ in São Paulo for five years.

c) They **go out** on Sundays.
   They have _____ several times this year.

d) I **study** in the morning.
   I have _____ during two mornings this week.

e) Joseph **plays** the piano very well.
   He has _____ in several recitals.

f) Jane **cooks** very well.
   She has _____ many delicious meals for me.

g) Bob **reads** a lot.
   He has _____ many books this year.

h) Mr Jones loves to **tell** stories.
   He has _____ us some funny ones.

**10.** Escolha a alternativa correta.

a) I _____ yesterday.
   (  ) went out
   (  ) have gone out

b) A thief _____ Mr Black's watch last night.
   (  ) has stolen
   (  ) stole

# Lesson 8 – Future tense

**John:** Next month **I will buy** a new car.

**Bill:** And **I will sell** my motorcycle. But **I won't buy** a new one because I have no money...

**FUTURE TENSE** (Tempo futuro)

1) Forma afirmativa: **verb to give** (dar)
   I will give (Eu darei)
   You will give (Você dará)
   He/She will give (Ele/Ela dará)
   We will give (Nós daremos)
   You will give (Vocês darão)
   They will give (Eles/Elas darão)

2) Forma interrogativa
   Will I give? (Eu darei?)
   Will you give? (Você dará?)
   Will he/she give? (Ele/Ela dará?)
   Will we give? (Nós daremos?)
   Will you give? (Vocês darão?)
   Will they give? (Eles/Elas darão?)

3) Forma negativa
   I will not give. I won't give
   (Eu não darei)
   You will not give. You won't give
   (Você não dará)
   He will not give. He won't give
   (Ele não dará)
   We will not give. We won't give
   (Nós não daremos)
   You will not give. You won't give
   (Vocês não darão)
   They will not give. They won't give
   (Eles/Elas não darão)

4) Forma abreviada do futuro:
   I'll give
   You'll give
   He'll give
   She'll give
   We'll give
   You'll give
   They'll give

**1.** Traduza o diálogo entre John e Bill.

**2.** Traduza os diálogos abaixo para o português.

- What **will you be**?
- **I will be** a football player And you?
- **I will be** a computer programmer.

It's 11 o'clock p.m.
Lisa calls her daughter.
- Nancy, it's very late! Come back home soon!
- Mom, the party is so good...
- What time **will you come back**?
- **I will come back** at midnight with my friends.

**3.** Observe o exemplo e responda às perguntas.

- What will they do tonight?
(study Science)
- **They will study Science.**

a) - What will you eat?
(rice and beans)

b) - What will you drink?
(water)

c) - What will you send to her?
(flowers)

d) - What will he buy?
(a magazine)

e) - What will you wear tonight?
(a black dress)

f) - What will she cook?
(a vegetable soup)

g) – What will Jane sing?
(an American rock'n roll)

h) – What will the farmer plant?
(wheat and corn)

i) – What will you give?
(a beautiful blouse)

**4.** Coloque as respostas do exercício anterior no futuro imediato. Observe o exemplo.

**They are going to study Science.**

a)

b)

c)

d)

e)

f)

g)

h)

i)

**5.** Use o futuro simples na forma abreviada. Observe o exemplo.

I will go with you.
**I'll go with you.**

a) I will call you later.

b) You will learn some new rules.

c) They will eat cake at the party.

d) We will come back soon.

e) She will watch the game on TV tonight.

f) He will sleep well.

**6.** Dê respostas bilíngues curtas e positivas (P) ou negativas (N). Observe os exemplos.

– Will you come late?
(Você voltará tarde?)
( P ) – **Yes, I will.**
(Sim, eu voltarei.)

– Will she wear a long dress?
(Ela usará um vestido longo?)
( N ) – **No, she won't.**
(Não, ela não usará.)

a) – Will you help me?
(Você me ajudará?)
( P )

b) – Will she go out tonight?
(Ela sairá esta noite?)
( P )

c) – Will you travel next week?
(Você vai viajar na próxima semana?)
( N )

d) – Will they watch the game?
(Eles vão assistir ao jogo?)
( N )

e) – Will you play with me?
(Você vai jogar comigo?)
( P )

**7.** Observe o exemplo e responda às perguntas.

– Who will plant wheat and corn?
(the farmer)
– **The farmer will plant wheat and corn.**

a) – Who will take care of my health? (the doctor)

b) – Who will take care of my teeth? (the dentist)

c) – Who will score the first goal? (Neymar)

d) – Who will catch the criminal? (the policeman)

e) – Who will come to the party tonight? (everybody)

f) – Who will lend you a pen? (Janice)

g) – Who will sweep the room? (John)

c) – Where will they pay their bills? (at the bank)

d) – Where will she take the bus? (on Nevada Street, at the bus stop)

e) – Where will Joe's family eat on weekends? (at Maximus restaurant)

f) – Where will you hide your money? (in a safe in my house)

**8.** Observe o exemplo e responda às perguntas.

– Where will they go tomorrow? (to the club)
– **They will go to the club.**

a) – Where will she go on Tuesday at 4 o'clock? (to the doctor's)

b) – Where will you buy fruit? (at the supermarket)

**9.** Observe o exemplo e responda às perguntas.

– When will you go to the dentist's? (tomorrow morning)
– **I will go to the dentist's tomorrow morning.**

a) – When will your mother go to the doctor's? (next month)

b) – When will be your birthday? (on the twenty-first of May)

c) – When will be the next meeting? (on the second of September)

d) – When will they go to France? (in June)

e) – When will you visit your parents? (on weekends)

f) – When will you leave to Manaus? (next week)

g) – When will the airplanes arrive? (tomorrow morning)

**10.** Escreva as frases na forma negativa abreviada. Observe o exemplo.

I will not pay the bill.
**I won't pay the bill.**

a) I will not leave before six.

b) People will not work at night.

c) They will not return late.

d) They will not work on Sundays.

## Dictation

**11.** Ouça com atenção o ditado que o professor vai apresentar e escreva.

**ANOTAÇÕES**

# Lesson 9 – Conditional tense

– Monica, I'm going to the beach tomorrow. **Would you like** to go with me?
– Of course. It's a great pleasure to enjoy your company, especially near the sea.

### CONDITIONAL TENSE (FUTURO DO PRETÉRITO)

**Verb to like** (gostar)

1) Forma afirmativa                                    (abreviada)
   I would like (Eu gostaria)                          I'd like
   You would like (Você gostaria)                      You'd like
   He/She would like (Ele/Ela gostaria)                He'd/She'd like
   We would like (Nós gostaríamos)                     We'd like
   You would like (Vocês gostariam)                    You'd like
   They would like (Eles/Elas gostariam)               They'd like

2) Forma interrogativa
   Would I like? (Eu gostaria?)
   Would you like? (Você gostaria?)
   Would he/she like? (Ele/Ela gostaria?)
   Would we like? (Nós gostaríamos?)
   Would you like? (Vocês gostariam?)
   Would they like? (Eles/Elas gostariam?)

3) Forma negativa                                              (abreviada)
   I would not like (Eu não gostaria)                          I'd not like/I wouldn't like
   You would not like (Você não gostaria)                      You'd not like/You wouldn't like
   He would not like (Ele não gostaria)                        He'd not like/He wouldn't like
   We would not like (Nós não gostaríamos)                     We'd not like/We wouldn't like
   You would not like (Vocês não gostariam)                    You'd not like/You wouldn't like
   They would not like (Eles/Elas não gostariam)               They'd not like/They wouldn't like

**1.** Traduza a conversa da foto na página anterior.

**2.** Observe o exemplo e responda às perguntas.

– How much coffee would you like to drink? (a little cup, please)
– **I would like to drink a little cup, please.**

a) – How much meat would she buy if she had money?
(10 kilograms of meat)

b) – How much sugar would you buy with ten dollars?
(25 kilograms)

c) – How much milk would Helen buy with ten dollars?
(15 packets)

d) – How much cheese would you buy with ten dollars?
(1 kilogram)

e) – How much ham would she buy with ten dollars?
(1 kilogram)

f) – How much salt would they buy with five dollars?
(10 kilograms)

**3.** Observe o exemplo e responda às perguntas.

– How many bottles of water would you like to take?
(10 bottles)
– **I would like to take ten bottles of water.**

a) – How many popular houses would they build with two million dollars?
(about a hundred houses)

b) – How many bananas would you like to eat? (four bananas)

c) – How many countries would you like to know in Europe? (five countries)

d) – How many milk cups would you like to drink?
(only one milk cup)

e) – How many toys would he like to buy? (two toys)

**4.** Responda às perguntas, use as expressões e palavras entre parênteses. Observe o exemplo.

– Where would you like to go?
(to the beach)
– **I would like to go to the beach.**

a) – Where would she like to buy clothes?
(at the shopping center)

b) – Where would you like to eat?
(at the Giardino restaurant)

c) – Where would they like to fish?
(at Porto Primavera Dam)

d) – Where would they like to swim?
(in the sea)

e) – Where would he like to walk?
(in the park)

f) – Where would they like to go?
(Bahia)

**5.** Responda às perguntas, use as expressões e palavras entre parênteses. Observe o exemplo.

– What would you like to eat? (a sandwich)
– I would like to eat a sandwich.

a) – What would you like to drink? (water)

b) – What country would you like to know? (France)

c) – What car would you like to buy? (a popular car)

d) – What magazine would you like to read? (National Geographic)

e) – What flat would they like to rent? (the flat number four)

f) – What would he like to give to his girlfriend? (a watch)

**6.** Escreva as perguntas seguindo o exemplo.

(coffee)
Would you like some coffee?

a) (cheese)

b) (ham)

c) (sugar)

d) (sweetener)

e) (milk)

f) (tea)

g) (salt)

h) (olive oil)

i) (vinegar)

> **EMPREGO DO IF (SE...), COM VERBOS NO TEMPO PRESENTE E TEMPO PASSADO**
>
> Observe:
> 1) Tempo presente
>    **If** you **study**, you **will pass** the examinations.
>    (Se você estudar, você passará nos exames.)
> 2) Tempo passado
>    **If** you **studied**, you **would pass** the examinations.
>    (Se você estudasse, você passaria nos exames.)
>
> Resumindo em forma de esquema:
> 1) If + present tense = future tense
> 2) If + past tense = conditional tense

**7.** Complete as frases empregando os verbos entre parênteses no **conditional tense** (futuro do pretérito) ou no **future tense** (futuro do presente).

a) Se João estudasse, ele **passaria** nos exames. (to pass)
If John studied, he _____ the examinations.

b) Se você frequentasse as aulas regularmente, **entenderia** Matemática. (to understand)
If you attended class regularly, you _____ Mathematics.

c) Se eu tiver tempo, **visitarei** você. (to visit)
If I have time, I _____ you.

d) Se ela tiver dinheiro, ela **comprará** aquele carro. (to buy)
If she has money, she _____ that car.

e) Se o professor explicasse a lição, nós a **entenderíamos**. (to understand)
If the teacher explained the lesson, we _____ it.

f) Se ela não estivesse doente, **viria** para a aula. (to come)
If she was not sick, she _____ to class.

g) Se eu tiver dinheiro, **pegarei** um táxi. (to take)
If I have money, I _____ a taxi.

h) Se nós tivéssemos o número de seu telefone, **telefonaríamos** para você. (to call)
If we had your telephone number, we _____ you.

**8.** Com base nas explicações anteriores, complete as frases empregando os verbos no **future tense** (will) ou no **conditional tense** (would).

a) If I **have** time, I _____ you tomorrow. (to visit)
(Se eu tiver tempo, **visitarei** você amanhã.)

b) If I **had** time, I _____ you. (to visit)
(Se eu tivesse tempo, **visitaria** você.)

c) If you **work**, you _____ much money. (to earn)
(Se você trabalhar, **ganhará** muito dinheiro.)

d) If she **worked**, she _____ a lot of money. (to earn)
(Se ela trabalhasse, **ganharia** muito dinheiro.)

e) If you **wait**, you _____ a beautiful show. (to see)
(Se você esperar, **verá** um lindo espetáculo.)

f) If she **waited**, she _____ a beautiful show. (to see)
(Se ela esperasse, **veria** um lindo espetáculo.)

**9.** Assinale a alternativa que, em inglês, corresponde à tradução das frases.

a) Se chover, nós não sairemos.

( ) If it rained, we will not go out.
( ) If it rains, we would not go out.
( ) If it rains, we will not go out.

b) Se você esperasse, eu iria com você.

( ) If you waited, I would go with you.
( ) If you wait, I will go with you.
( ) If you wait, I would go with you. you.

> **Observação:**
>
> Nas orações com **If** (se) usamos **were** em todas as pessoas, porém na linguagem informal admite-se **was** (1ª e 3ª pessoas).
>
> A única expressão obrigatória é:
> **If I were you:** Se eu fosse você.

**11.** Traduza para o português as frases do exercício anterior.

**10.** Relacione as orações de acordo com o sentido.

a) If she won the lottery
b) If you press this button
c) If I were rich
d) If they want to pass
e) If I were you
f) If they took a taxi

( ) they will have to study more.
( ) she would travel around the world.
( ) I would accept the invitation.
( ) they would get to the airport in time.
( ) I would help poor people.
( ) you will turn the radio off.

# Lesson 10 – Passive voice

The National Congress Building was designed by Oscar Niemeyer, who follows the style of modern Brazilian architecture. The building is situated in the Monumental Axis, the main avenue of Brazil's capital.

The Latin American Memorial was opened in 1989. The architectural complex was designed by Oscar Niemeyer.
It is a monument to the cultural, political, economic and social development in Latin America.

**PASSIVE VOICE**

**Verb to be = past participle of the main verb**

Example:

The National Congress Building **was designed** by Oscar Niemeyer.

(O edifício do Congresso Nacional foi projetado por Oscar Niemeyer.)

**1.** Traduza os textos acima.

**2.** Observe os exemplos e passe as frases para a voz passiva. Observe que os verbos variam de acordo com o tempo verbal na voz ativa.

The postman **delivers** letters every day.
Letters **are delivered** by the postman every day.

The postman **delivered** some letters yesterday.
Some letters **were delivered** by the postman yesterday.

The postman **will deliver** some letters tomorrow.
Some letters **will be delivered** by the postman tomorrow.

a) The police **arrested** some criminals.

b) Larissa **washes** the hair every day.

c) Bob **will paint** the house next year.

d) The government **built** many popular houses.

e) The teacher **solved** the problem in class.

**3.** Escolha a alternativa correta e complete as frases na voz passiva.

a) The goalkeeper will catch the ball.
The ball _____ by the goalkeeper.
( ) is caught
( ) was caught
( ) will be caught

b) Sara found the keys.
The keys _____ by Sara.
( ) are found
( ) were found
( ) will be found

c) A lot of people admire the football player Ronaldinho.
The football player Ronaldinho _____ by a lot of people.
( ) is admired
( ) was admired
( ) will be admired

d) Nancy bought a lot of apples last week.
A lot of apples _____ by Nancy last week.
( ) are bought
( ) were bought
( ) will be bough

e) A strange boy followed the girl.
The girl _____ by a strange boy.
( ) is followed
( ) was followed
( ) will be followed

**4.** Ordene as palavras e forme as frases na voz passiva.

a) car – imported – This – was – Germany – from

b) house – by – was – the – fire – destroyed – The

c) students – examined – The teachers – by – the – will be

d) car – yesterday – The – sold – was – red

e) food – served – in – Delicious – is – this – restaurant

f) letters – by – Several – delivered – postman – were – the

g) were – terrorists – Twin Towers – The – by – destroyed

h) meeting – cancelled – The – the – was – actor – by

**5.** Observe o exemplo e mude as sentenças para a voz passiva (**passive voice**). Os verbos estão no tempo presente (**present tense**).

The doctor **examines** the patient.
**The patient is examined by the doctor.**

a) The gardener **plants** flowers.

b) The maid **cleans** the windows.

c) Trucks **transport** heavy loads.

d) The milkman **delivers** milk every day.

e) A lot of people **admire** that singer.

f) The boy **closes** the door.

**6.** Observe o exemplo e mude as sentenças para a voz passiva (**passive voice**). Os verbos estão no passado (**past tense**).

Jane **prepared** the food.
**The food was prepared by Jane.**

a) Mary **received** the letter.

b) My sister **opened** the door.

c) The pupils **answered** the questions.

d) The police **arrested** the thief.

e) Monica **invited** John.

f) The teacher **corrected** the exercises.

**7.** Observe o exemplo e mude as frases para a voz passiva.

The maid will clean the house.
**The house will be cleaned by the maid.**

a) Jane will prepare a good meal.

b) The teacher will explain the lesson.

c) Mary will invite a lot of people.

d) The pupils will correct the exercises.

e) The editor will publish a lot of books.

f) The police will arrest the thief.

g) Our company will deliver the merchandise.

**ANOTAÇÕES**

# Lesson 11 – Question tags

**QUESTION TAG** (PERGUNTA NO FINAL DA FRASE)

Ao terminarmos uma frase, afirmativa ou negativa, muitas vezes acrescentamos uma pergunta rápida para ter a confirmação do que dissemos antes. A essa pergunta rápida chamamos de **question tag**, exemplo:

a) She is beautiful, **isn't she**?
   (Ela é bonita, não é?)
b) They are not rich, **are they**?
   (Eles não são ricos, são?)

Quando a declaração inicial for afirmativa, a **question tag** será negativa, porém, se a declaração inicial for negativa, a **question tag** será afirmativa. Veja outros exemplos:

The house is large, **isn't it**?
(A casa é grande, não é?)
They were not rich, **were they**?
(Eles não eram ricos, eram?)
You like coffee, **don't you**?
(Você gosta de café, não gosta?)
You don't speak Japanese, **do you**?
(Você não fala japonês, fala?)

> He is an American singer, isn't he?

**1.** Traduza a fala da foto acima.

**2.** Observe os exemplos e complete com a **question tag** apropriada. Lembre-se de que a **question tag** será formada por um verbo auxiliar na forma abreviada (**to be, to have, to do** ou **modal**) + pronome.

It is very cold today, **isn't it**?
The test was easy, **wasn't it**?
They were rich, **weren't they**?

a) She has beautiful eyes, _____?

b) You can go with me, _____?

c) She could help you, ?

d) The problems aren't difficult, ?

e) Paula isn't English, ?

f) The oranges aren't ripe, ?

g) She isn't at home, ?

h) They haven't read the book, ?

i) It isn't raining, ?

j) They weren't at the party, ?

k) George is a good friend, ?

l) It was a good game, ?

m) Your parents are at home, ?

n) She can help you, ?

o) They can't see you, ?

**3.** Observe os exemplos e complete as frases com **question tags** apropriadas.

You speak English, **don't you**?
She speaks English, **doesn't she**?
They lived on a farm, **didn't they**?

a) You don't speak English, ?

b) She doesn't speak English, ?

c) They didn't live on a farm, ?

d) Mary loves you, ?

e) You love your parents, ?

f) Meg loved her garden, ?

g) Nancy doesn't play football, ?

h) They don't know my country, ?

i) You didn't pay the bill, ?

j) They work hard, ?

k) He works in an office, ?

l) She sells magazines, ?

m) Marcel bought a new car, ?

n) Mary didn't wash the plates, ?

o) She didn't change her dress, ?

**4.** Leia o texto em voz alta e diga oralmente o que você entendeu.

**GUESSING GAME**

Let's see who can discover an important person that I'm thinking...

**Joe:** She is a woman, **isn't she**?
**Paul:** No, she is not a woman.
**Lucy:** He lives in Brazil, **doesn't he**?
**Paul:** No, he doesn't live in Brazil.
**Monica:** He isn't a singer, **is he**?
**Paul:** No, he is not.
**Nanci:** He is alive, **isn't he**?
**Paul:** No, he is dead.
**George:** He isn't American, **is he**?
**Paul:** No, he is not.
**Robert:** He is German, **isn't he**?
**Paul:** Right! He is German.
**Lucy:** He was a scientist, **wasn't he**?
**Paul:** Yes, he was a great scientist.
**Lucy:** I know his name... His name is Albert Einstein.
**Paul:** Great! Correct!

**5.** Observe os exemplos no **future tense** e **conditional tense** e depois faça os exercícios.

They will go to the park, **won't they**?
They will not go to the park, **will they**?
She would marry him, **wouldn't she**?

a) She would not marry him, ?

b) She would dance with him, ?

c) They will meet us at the station, ?

d) They will be in class tomorrow, ?

e) He won't be back until seven, ?

f) Mary will plant some flowers in the spring, ?

g) John won't call you at night, ?

h) You wouldn't tell the truth, ?

i) Bob won't be absent from class tomorrow, ?

j) They wouldn't travel by plane, ?

k) She wouldn't come in the evening, ?

l) You wouldn't help her, ?

**Observação:**

As frases iniciadas por verbo no imperativo podem também terminar com **will you** ou **would you**:
Close the door, **will you**?
(Feche a porta, está bem?)
Bring me something to eat, **would you**?
(Traga-me alguma coisa para comer, está bem?)

# Lesson 12 – Pronouns

**Alexander Fleming** was a Scottish scientist **who** discovered penicillin.

**Penicillin** is a kind of antibiotic **which** kills many harmful bacteria.

Bacteria are one-celled living beings **that** you can see only with a microscope and **which** can cause many diseases.

PRONOMES RELATIVOS

**Who:** que (refere-se a pessoas)
Alexander Fleming was a scientist **who** discovered penicillin.
(Alexander Fleming foi um cientista que descobriu a penicilina.)
**That:** que
Take the book **that** is on the table.
(Pegue o livro que está sobre a mesa.)
**Which:** que (denota escolha)
Take the ball **which** is red.
(Pegue a bola que é vermelha.)
**Whose:** cujo, cuja, cujos, cujas.
The man **whose** shirt is blue is my father.
(O homem cuja camisa é azul é meu pai.)
**Whom:** a quem, de quem, para quem, com quem...
The girl **whom** John married is my sister.
(A garota com quem João se casou é minha irmã.)
**Where:** no qual, na qual, onde...
The house **where** I lived was in front of the beach.
(A casa onde eu vivia ficava em frente à praia.)
**When:** em que, no qual...
I remember the day **when** you were born.
(Eu me lembro do dia em que você nasceu.)

**1.** Traduza o texto sobre Fleming.

**2.** Complete as frases com pronomes relativos.

a) The boy _____ stole my watch was put in prision.

b) I've just called my brother _____ lives in Rio.

c) The woman _____ bought my house is very rich.

d) The factory _____ they work belongs to Mr Freiner.

e) That is the store _____ they work.

f) The house _____ I was born was destroyed.

g) The book _____ you are talking about is very interesting.

h) The teacher _____ son is Paul lives near me.

i) The girl _____ you gave flowers is my sister.

j) The pilot _____ car is red won the race.

k) The men _____ are playing tennis are my friends.

l) The girl _____ sits near me is always smiling.

m) Did you receive the e-mail _____ I sent you?

n) I miss my girlfriend _____ is studying in France.

o) The flat _____ I live is very comfortable.

p) This is the artist _____ name I can't remember.

q) Do you remember the date _____ Brazil became champion?

r) I like to be among _____ people _____ are always happy.

a) That is the boy. He reads very well.

b) People live in big cities. They are deprived of a healthy environment.

**3.** Passe para o inglês:

a) A casa em que vivemos é confortável.

b) Aquela é a mulher cujo marido você conhece.

c) There is a man outside. He wants to see you.

d) I know the girl. She married Bob last year.

> **Observação:**
> O pronome relativo **who** tem sempre como antecedente uma pessoa e funciona como sujeito.

e) The man was following us. He is a policeman.

**4.** Una as duas orações num único período por meio do pronome relativo **who**. Observe o exemplo.

The girl is my friend. She called me yesterday.
The girl who called me yesterday is my friend.

> **Observação:**
> O pronome relativo **that** pode ter como antecedente pessoa, animal ou coisa. Pode funcionar como sujeito ou objeto; por isso, é muito usado, podendo substituir o pronome relativo **who**.

**5.** Observe o exemplo e una as duas orações por meio do pronome relativo **that**.

He is the boy. He reads very well.
**He is the boy that reads very well.**

a) People live in big cities.
   They are deprived of a healthy environment.

b) There is a man outside.
   He wants to see you.

c) I know the player.
   He scored that goal.

d) I bought a car.
   It is very comfortable.

e) The present is very pretty.
   You sent me yesterday.

f) The book is very good.
   I read it last year.

g) The bus was very old.
   We took it yesterday.

h) The animal is the horse.
   I like best.

> **Observação:**
> O pronome relativo **which** tem como antecedente coisas ou animais. Normalmente, podemos substituir o pronome relativo **that** por **which**.

**6.** Observe o exemplo e una as duas orações por meio do pronome **which**:

I bought a car. It cost a lot.
**I bought a car which cost a lot.**

a) That's the house. You saw it yesterday.

b) She lent me a book. It is very interesting.

c) Yesterday I saw a film. It was very amusing.

d) I like the picture. It is in the living room.

e) The cat is an Angora. It is on the sofa.

**Observação:**

O pronome relativo **whom** tem como antecedente uma pessoa. É objeto e pode vir precedido de preposição.

**7.** Observe o exemplo e una as duas orações num único período por meio do pronome relativo **whom**:

I saw a man in the house yesterday. The man was a thief.

The man whom I saw in the house yesterday was a thief.

a) The patient is very ill. The doctor visited him yesterday.

b) The girl is my friend. You spoke to her.

c) The boy is my cousin. You met him yesterday.

**Observação:**

O pronome relativo **whose** se refere a um substantivo que vem logo depois dele. Significa: cujo, cuja, cujos, cujas, do qual, dos quais.

**8.** Observe o exemplo e una as duas orações num único período por meio do pronome relativo **whose**:

I know a man. His wife is a teacher.
I know a man whose wife is a teacher.

a) This is the book. The pages are dirty.

b) This is the singer. You heard his voice yesterday.

c) This is the cowboy. His name is Blackhorn.

d) This is the man. I admire his character.

e) That is the girl. Her mother is a pilot.

**Observação:**

Podemos omitir o pronome relativo se o verbo da oração subordinada já tiver um sujeito. Exemplo:
This is the girl that **I like** best.
This is the girl ...... **I like** best.
(O verbo **like** já tem um sujeito, **I**; portanto, podemos suprimir o **that**.)

**9.** Observe o exemplo e omita o pronome relativo sempre que for possível:

The boy that you spoke to is my friend.
**The boy you spoke to is my friend.**

a) The girl whom you want to see is here.

b) The book which I was reading is very interesting.

c) The present that I got yesterday is a wonderful watch.

d) The car that I like best is a green Fiat.

e) The girl whom you saw at the movies is my cousin.

**10.** Observe as figuras e o modelo e responda às questões.

> **Observação:**
>
> Usamos **which** (qual) em vez de **what** (qual) quando temos de escolher uma entre várias coisas ou opções:

a) – Here are a strawberry and orange ice creams. Which do you prefer? (The strawberry)

– Here are a banana and an apple.
Which do you prefer?
(the apple)
– I prefer the apple.
– I don't like bananas.

b) – Here are two kind of flowers: red and yellow flowers. Which do you prefer? (red)

d) – Here are two cars.
A big and a small car.
Which do you prefer? (big)

f) – In the clothes hanger there
are white and green blouses.
Which do you prefer? (green)

e) – Here are two means of
transportation: a motorcycle
and a horse. Which do
you prefer? (the horse)

**ANOTAÇÕES**

# Lesson 13 – Gerund

- Do you like dancing?
- No, I prefer staying here looking at people.
- Why don't you dance with me?
- Because I like dancing in the crowd.

**Attention: Use gerund after these verbs. Don't use infinitive**

| | |
|---|---|
| to admit | She **admitted driving** too fast. |
| to avoid | We couldn't **avoid doing** that. |
| to appreciate | I'll **appreciate hearing** something from you. |
| to consider | I am **considering selling** my house. |
| to deny | She **denied going out**. |
| to dislike | She **dislikes going out** without you. |
| to enjoy | I **enjoy playing** football. |
| to finish | I have **finished doing** my homework. |
| to risk | You shouldn't **risk driving** in that way. |
| to stop | I **stopped reading** that book. |

**These verbs are followed by infinitive or gerund**

| | |
|---|---|
| to begin | I **begin to work (working)** today. |
| to cease | The wind **ceased to blow (blowing)**. |
| to continue | I'll **continue to work (working)** in that department. |
| to forget | I **forgot to do (doing)** my homework. |
| to hate | I **hate to get up (getting up)** early. |
| to intend | She **intends to go (going)** there by car. |
| to like | She **likes to dance (dancing)** at my club. |
| to love | She **loves to drink (drinking)** milk shake. |
| to neglect | She usually **neglects to go (going)** to the dentist. |
| to prefer | I **prefer to swim (swimming)** in the afternoon. |
| to remember | I **remember to take (taking)** two boxes. |
| to start | I **started to read (reading)** this book yesterday. |

**1.** Traduza o diálogo da fotografia da página anterior.

**2.** Coloque os verbos no gerúndio (**gerund form**).

a) I don't **like** _____ ties.
   (to wear)

b) I don't **like** _____ late.
   (to come back)

c) Many people **prefer** _____ instead of _____. (to walk – to drive)

d) He **forgot** _____ another pen. (to buy)

e) I don't **like** _____ those sad days. (to remember)

f) She **enjoys** _____ in the morning. (to walk)

**3.** Complete as frases com os verbos no gerúndio.

hurting – crying – walking – opening

a) The baby started _____.

b) Try to avoid _____ your fellows in the football game.

c) We talked about _____ a new shop.

d) After _____ a long time we arrived at the station.

> **Observação:**
> Use gerúndio depois de preposição.
> She left **without saying** goodbye.
> She buys milk **before going** home.
> They are thinking **of coming** back.
> I am fond **of playing** football.
> I'm tired **of reading**.
> (Estou cansado de ler.)
> A pen is used **for writing**.
> (Uma caneta é usada para escrever.)

**4.** Relacione as duas colunas e complete as frases com gerúndio. Observe o exemplo.

| | |
|---|---|
| knife | painting |
| needle | climbing |
| pen | writing |
| towel | sewing |
| key | cutting |
| ladder | sticking |
| glue | drying |
| painter's brush | eating |
| fork | opening and locking |

A **knife** is used for **cutting**.

a) A pen is used _____.
b) A ladder is used _____.
c) A towel is used _____.
d) A fork is used _____.
e) Glue is used _____.
f) A key is used _____.
g) A needle is used _____.
h) A painter's brush is used _____.

**5.** Use gerúndio depois da preposição. Observe o exemplo.

I am fond of (dance).
**I am fond of dancing.**

a) I am tired of (work).

b) I'm interested in (help) people.

c) He had no intention of (hurt) you.

d) The teacher spoke about (save) water.

e) The girl was tired after (walk) two kilometers.

f) She left without (say) goodbye.

g) Thank you for (come) to my party.

h) He is interested in (buy) a new car.

# Additional texts

**1.** Leia com atenção os textos e traduza-os.

**I HAVE A DREAM**

"I have a dream that one day men will rise up and come to see that they are made to live together as brothers."

Martin Luther King Jr. was a leader who wanted equal rights for black and white people in the United States. He received The Nobel Peace Prize in 1964 and was murdered in 1968.

**Ever:** Love and fraternity
**Never:** Discrimination

**YOUNG PEOPLE**

A lot of young people think that their families do not understand their problems.

Young people generally make their decisions alone or with the help of a friend of the same age.

Very often this happens because there is no communication between parents and children.

Parents, sometimes, have no time to talk with their children, and boys and girls move and leave their parents.

There are, of course, different solutions for this situation. For example:

Parents must talk frankly to their children and try to understand their problems.

**2.** Responda de acordo com o texto.

a) Very often there is no communication between parents and children. What is the solution for that situation?

b) What do many young people think?

**3.** Escreva **true** (verdadeiro) ou **false** (falso) de acordo com o texto.

(　　　) Parents, sometimes, have no time to talk with their children.

(　　　) Young people don't make decisions with the help of a friend.

**MENTAL HEALTH**

When your body is well, you have physical health.

When your mind is well, you have mental health.

Mental health is very important.

What is it necessary to have mental health?

- To love and be loved.
- To meet friends.
- To control our feelings.
- To look at the future with hope.
- To recognize our limitations.
- To face the problems and live in reality.
- To have a hobby.
- To practice sports and physical exercises.
- To discover our special qualities.
- To have spare time and vacations.
- To sleep well.

**ANOTAÇÕES**

**4.** Leia o texto com atenção e faça sua tradução.

**WATER**
Rain falls on the land and forms little rivers that generally flow to sea.
Man can stop rivers and form artificial lakes to provide water in agriculture, cities, etc.
Water comes to our houses through pipes. Pipes take water to sinks, showers, toilets, washing machines, etc.
Today the world has a great lack of water, so everyone must save it.

**NATURE**
It is nice to live in contact with nature. Nature is beautiful and a source of life. Observing nature attentively, we note that every being depends on the others. Nature gives everything to man. Why destroy it? It's necessary to love and protect nature so that it can be a source of life forever.
The Earth doesn't belong to man; it's man that belongs to the Earth. The Earth is our mother, the rivers are our brothers and the forests are our sisters. The authorities must find a way to avoid pollution and preserve nature. And you, too!

**5.** Responda de acordo com o texto.

a) Do rivers generally flow to the sea?

b) How does water come to our houses?

c) Why must everyone save water?

**6.** Escreva (**true**) para verdadeiro ou (**false**) para falso, de acordo com o texto.

(　　　)Rains don't form rivers.
(　　　)Rain forms rivers.
(　　　)Everyone must save water.

**7.** Responda de acordo com o texto.

a) Is it nice to live in contact with nature?

b) Is nature a source of life?

c) Does the Earth belong to man?

d) What must the authorities do?

e) And you, what must you do?

**8.** Traduza as frases para o português.

a) Every being depends on the others.

b) Protect nature. It can be a source of life forever.

c) Everyone must protect nature.

d) Nature gives everything to man.

e) Avoid pollution!

f) Man belongs to the Earth.

---

**TOURISM**

Tourism is a way of knowing new places, different people, other customs, traditions, folklore and local food. One can travel for pleasure, on business, for reasons of health, on holiday, etc.

When you travel as a tourist you can buy original things from other places and countries.

Tourism is leisure and culture.

Today we have the Ecotourism that is a new way of staying in contact with nature and its beauties.

**9.** Responda de acordo com o texto.

a) What is tourism?

b) What is Ecotourism?

**FITNESS AND HEALTH**

Getting in shape is a constant preoccupation for millions of people today. Regular exercises are part of their daily life. While some of them swim, run or cycle, others exercise in gyms or do aerobics.

People who practice regular exercises are healthier than unfit people, especially those who drink, smoke or take drugs. This fact is confirmed by recent medical researches.

Today there is a great pressure on men and women to look young, beautiful and attractive.

**10.** Complete a resposta de acordo com o texto.

What is a constant preoccupation for millions of people today?

A constant preoccupation for millions of people has been to

**11.** Escreva (**true**) para verdadeiro ou (**false**) para falso.

a) People who practice regular exercises are healthier than people who smoke, drink or take drugs. (           )

b) Physical exercises don't make us healthy. (           )

**12.** Complete a frase com base no texto.

Today there is a great pressure on men and women to look

**A JOB AGENCY**

Are you unemployed? Are you going to change your job? In our agency there are many jobs for you and your friends. Here they are! Look:

**Teachers** of Mathematics, Geography and History;

**English teacher** (a native speaker of English);

**Teachers** (three girls, with some experience with children: a job for five weeks);

**Interpreter** (a girl speaking English and Japanese: a job for two weeks);

**Reporter** (for a new magazine);

**Photographer** (with some experience in sports);

**Cook**, **waiter** and **waitress** (with experience in Chinese restaurants);

**Ten doctors** and **twenty nurses** (for a new hospital);

**Carpenter** (for two weeks);

**Gardener** (for a week);

**Workers** (We need a lot of workers for a new shoe factory).

Come to our agency! We are waiting for you! We have a good job for you!

**13.** Consulte o vocabulário no final deste caderno e traduza o texto.

**ANOTAÇÕES**

**POP MUSIC**

**Martin:** Why do young people love pop music so much?

**John:** Because:
- music excite them;
- music is a global language;
- it's social – it brings young people together in dancing clubs;
- it brings people together, destroying all barriers: age, color, religion, sex and social class;
- it gives pleasure to millions of people.

**14.** Consulte o vocabulário no final deste caderno e traduza o texto.

**MAINTENANCE**

For a lot of people a car is a necessity. However, cars need a regular maintenance such as to repair and replace damaged parts. The driver must check constantly the components of the car: brake, electrical system, wheel alignment, oil, the water in the radiator, tires, etc. The seat belts must be always clean and in good conditions of use.

Remember: Alcohol does not combine with the responsibility of driving.

**SEAT BELTS – SAFETY FOR YOU**

Seat belts are very important safety components in a car.

They reduce injuries and deaths in any speed.

Lap and shoulder belts absorb and reduce the impact. Thousands of drivers and passengers have been saved because of the seat belts.

Children must travel on the back seats and use belts too.

Remember: seat belt is a guarantee for your life! Don't forget it! Believe in it!... and have a nice trip!

**15.** What are your favorite musicians?

**16.** Consulte o vocabulário no final deste caderno e traduza o texto:

**ANOTAÇÕES**

# Fun time – Divirta-se aprendendo

Answers that start with G

**1.** The answer to each question starts with G. The picture above each description can help you.

A piece of ground for raising flowers.

A place where we keep our car.

A musical instrument with six strings.

**2.** Write words that sound alike. (Escreva palavras que tenham som semelhante.)

a) look:

b) lake:

c) cat:

d) fox:

e) hen:

f) pot:

g) line:

h) small:

**3.** What's the girl's name?

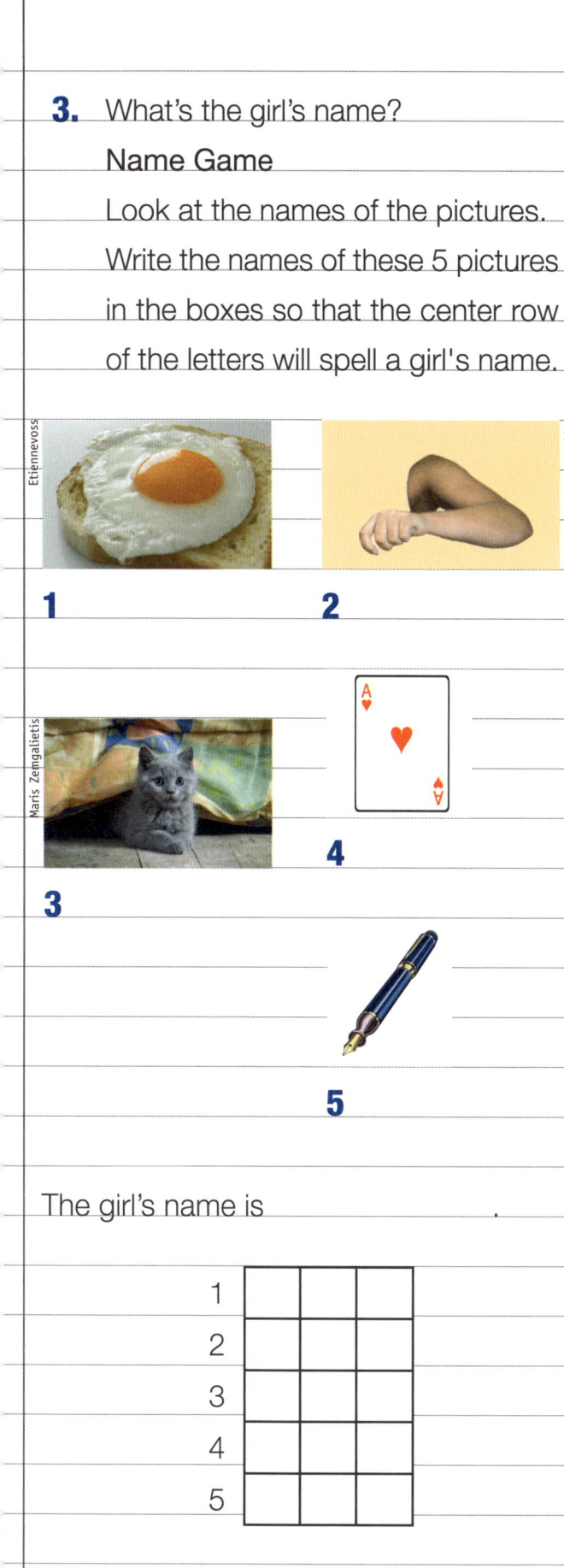

**Name Game**

Look at the names of the pictures. Write the names of these 5 pictures in the boxes so that the center row of the letters will spell a girl's name.

1. 
2. 
3. 
4. 
5. 

The girl's name is _____.

**4.** Alphabet soup.

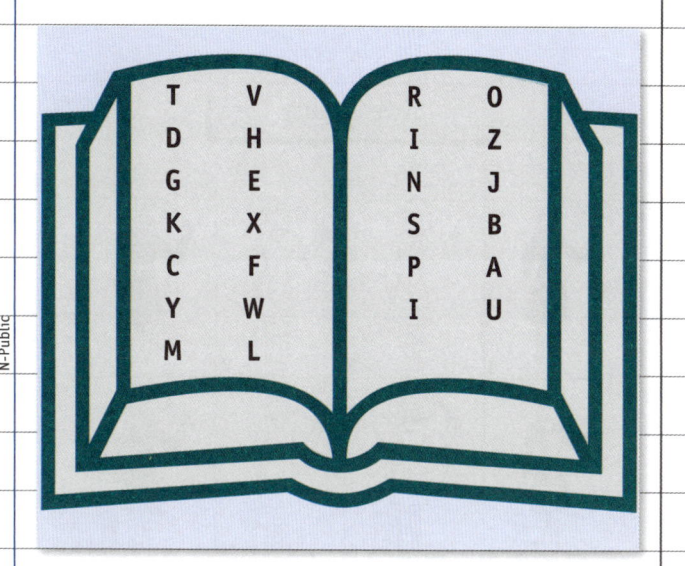

```
T  V    R  O
D  H    I  Z
G  E    N  J
K  X    S  B
C  F    P  A
Y  W    I  U
M  L
```

One alphabet letter is missing in the book above and another letter appears twice. Which are the letters?

**5.** Unscramble the name of these animals beginning with H.

erah
heros
neh

**6.** Unscramble the letters of these numbers.

eno
tow
net

119

**7.** Look at the images below and answer.

Sixteen girls

a) There are sixteen girls. Are they all the same?
( ) Yes    ( ) No

b) How many girls are wearing black dresses?

c) How many girls are wearing white dresses?

d) How many girls are holding flags?

e) How many girls are wearing hats?

f) How many girls are standing on a box?

g) Can you say which girl is this?
She is standing on a box.
She is wearing a white dress.
She is holding a flag.
She is not wearing a hat.
She is the girl number          .

h) Can you say which girl is this?
She is wearing a black dress.
She is not standing on a box.
She is wearing a hat.
She is holding a flag.
She is the girl number

i) Can you guess which girl is this?
She is wearing a black dress.
She is not wearing a hat.

She is not standing on a box.
She is not holding a flag.
She is the girl number

j) Can you guess which girl is this?
She is wearing a white dress.
She is wearing a white hat.
She is not standing on a box.
She is not holding a flag.
She is the girl number

**8.** Write the opposites of the words below. Use these opposites.

> obey – arrive – dirty – hot – can't – night – old – bad

clean
good
day
can
return
new
disobey
cold

**9.** Complete the words writing the missing vowels.

a) Sh wnt t th prk.

b) Th grl knw th lssn.

c) Jhn plyd tnns ystrdy.

d) Thy spk nglsh wll.

**ANOTAÇÕES**

**SCRAMBLED WORDS FOR BREAKFAST**

When I come to the table in the morning for my breakfast I generally have **KMIL** and **FOFEEC** with **RADBE**, **UTTBER**, **EECHSE** and **MAJ**.
My mother likes black **FOFEEC** with **CUITBISS** or **TASOT** with some **UTTBER**.
My father usually has **MAJ** with **TASOT** but sometimes he likes to eat fried **SEGG** and **CONBA**.
My sister loves **KESFLACORN** with **KMIL**, but sometimes she has **HURTYOG** or **ITFRU CEJUI**.

cornflakes   jam

bread

**10.** Com o auxílio do vocabulário, escreva abaixo o texto em inglês, com as palavras desembaralhadas:

## LIST OF IRREGULAR VERBS

| Infinitive | Translation | Simple Past | Past Participle |
|---|---|---|---|
| 1. to be | ser, estar | was, were | been |
| 2. to become | tornar-se | becam e | become |
| 3. to begin | começar | began | begun |
| 4. to blow | soprar | blew | blown |
| 5. to break | quebrar | broke | broken |
| 6. to bring | trazer | brought | brought |
| 7. to build | construir | built | built |
| 8. to burst | arrebentar | burst | burst |
| 9. to buy | comprar | bought | bought |
| 10. to cast | arremessar | cast | cast |
| 11. to catch | pegar | caught | caught |
| 12. to choose | escolher | chose | chosen |
| 13. to come | vir | came | come |
| 14. to cost | custar | cost | cost |
| 15. to cut | cortar | cut | cut |
| 16. to deal | negociar | dealt | dealt |
| 17. to dig | cavar | dug | dug |
| 18. to do | fazer | did | done |
| 19. to draw | desenhar | drew | drawn |
| 20. to dream | sonhar | dreamt (dreamed) | dreamt (dreamed) |
| 21. to drink | beber | drank | drunk |
| 22. to drive | dirigir | drove | driven |
| 23. to eat | comer | ate | eaten |
| 24. to fall | cair | fell | fallen |
| 25. to feed | alimentar | fed | fed |
| 26. to feel | sentir | felt | felt |
| 27. to fight | lutar | fought | fought |
| 28. to find | encontrar | found | found |
| 29. to fly | voar | flew | flown |
| 30. to forget | esquecer | forgot | forgotten |
| 31. to freeze | gelar | froze | frozen |
| 32. to get | conseguir | got | got (gotten) |
| 33. to give | dar | gave | given |

| # | Infinitive | Tradução | Past | Past Participle |
|---|---|---|---|---|
| 34. | to go | ir | went | gone |
| 35. | to grow | crescer | grew | grown |
| 36. | to hang | pendurar | hung | hung |
| 37. | to have | ter | had | had |
| 38. | to hear | ouvir | heard | heard |
| 39. | to hide | esconder | hid | hidden |
| 40. | to hit | bater | hit | hit |
| 41. | to hold | segurar | held | held |
| 42. | to hurt | machucar | hurt | hurt |
| 43. | to keep | guardar | kept | kept |
| 44. | to know | saber | knew | known |
| 45. | to lay | pôr, deitar | laid | laid |
| 46. | to lead | guiar | led | led |
| 47. | to learn | aprender | learnt (learned) | learnt (learned) |
| 48. | to leave | deixar, partir | left | left |
| 49. | to lend | emprestar | lent | lent |
| 50. | to let | deixar, permitir | let | let |
| 51. | to lie | mentir, jazer | lay | lain |
| 52. | to light | iluminar | lit (lighted) | lit (lighted) |
| 53. | to lose | perder | lost | lost |
| 54. | to make | fazer, fabricar | made | made |
| 55. | to mean | significar | meant | meant |
| 56. | to meet | encontrar-se com | met | met |
| 57. | to pay | pagar | paid | paid |
| 58. | to put | pôr | put | put |
| 59. | to read | ler | read | read |
| 60. | to ride | cavalgar | rode | ridden |
| 61. | to ring | tocar a campainha | rang | rung |
| 62. | to rise | erguer-se | rose | risen |
| 63. | to run | correr | ran | run |
| 64. | to say | dizer | said | said |
| 65. | to see | ver | saw | seen |
| 66. | to sell | vender | sold | sold |
| 67. | to send | enviar | sent | sent |
| 68. | to set | colocar, fixar | set | set |
| 69. | to shake | sacudir | shook | shaken |
| 70. | to shine | brilhar | shone (shined) | shone (shined) |

| # | Infinitive | Tradução | Past Simple | Past Participle |
|---|---|---|---|---|
| 71. | to shoot | atirar, disparar | shot | shot |
| 72. | to show | mostrar | showed | shown (showed) |
| 73. | to shut | fechar | shut | shut |
| 74. | to sing | cantar | sang | sung |
| 75. | to sink | afundar | sank | sunk |
| 76. | to sit | sentar | sat | sat |
| 77. | to sleep | dormir | slept | slept |
| 78. | to slide | escorregar | slid | slid |
| 79. | to slit | fender, rachar | slit | slit |
| 80. | to smell | cheirar | smelt | smelt |
| 81. | to speak | falar | spoke | spoken |
| 82. | to speed | apressar-se | sped (speeded) | sped (speeded) |
| 83. | to spend | gastar | spent | spent |
| 84. | to spoil | estragar | spoilt | spoilt |
| 85. | to spread | espalhar | spread | spread |
| 86. | to spring | saltar | sprang | sprung |
| 87. | to stand | ficar de pé | stood | stood |
| 88. | to steal | roubar | stole | stolen |
| 89. | to strike | bater | struck | struck |
| 90. | to swear | jurar | swore | sworn |
| 91. | to sweep | varrer | swept | swept |
| 92. | to swim | nadar | swam | swum |
| 93. | to swing | balançar | swung | swung |
| 94. | to take | tomar | took | taken |
| 95. | to teach | ensinar | taught | taught |
| 96. | to tell | contar, dizer | told | told |
| 97. | to think | pensar | thought | thought |
| 98. | to throw | arremessar | threw | thrown |
| 99. | to understand | entender | understood | understood |
| 100. | to wake | acordar | woke | woken |
| 101. | to wear | vestir, usar | wore | worn |
| 102. | to wed | desposar | wed (wedded) | wed (wedded) |
| 103. | to wet | umedecer | wet | wet |
| 104. | to win | ganhar, vencer | won | won |
| 105. | to wring | espremer, torcer | wrung | wrung |
| 106. | to write | escrever | wrote | written |

# General vocabulary

**A**

**a lot**: uma porção, muito, muitos
**a week**: por semana
**a week ago**: uma semana atrás
**about**: sobre, a respeito de, aproximadamente
**above**: acima de, no alto
**absent**: ausente
**accept**: aceitar
**according**: de acordo
**accustomed**: acostumado
**ace**: ás
**act**: encenar, representar
**activity**: atividade
**add**: somar
**addict**: viciado, dependente
**addiction**: dependência
**address**: endereço
**admit**: admitir
**advantage**: vantagem
**advertising**: anúncio
**advice**: conselho
**afraid of**: com medo de
**after**: depois de
**after all**: afinal de contas
**afternoon**: tarde
**again**: de novo
**age**: idade
**agency**: agência
**ago**: atrás, antes
**agree**: concordar
**aim**: fim, finalidade, objetivo
**airplane**: avião
**alarm-clock**: despertador
**alignment**: alinhamento
**alive**: vivo
**all**: tudo, todos, todas
**all over the world**: em todo o mundo
**all right**: tudo bem, tudo certo
**almost**: quase
**alone**: só, sozinho
**already**: já
**also**: também
**always**: sempre
**among**: entre (entre muitos)
**amplify**: amplificar
**amusing**: divertido
**and that's why**: e é por isso que
**angry**: bravo, furioso
**another**: outro
**answer**: responder; resposta
**anxious**: ansioso, nervoso
**any**: algum, nenhum, qualquer
**any more**: não mais
**anyone**: nenhum, alguém, qualquer um
**anything**: nada; algo
**anything else**: algo mais
**anywhere**: em qualquer lugar,
**appear**: aparecer
**apple**: maçã

**are**: são, estão
**are there?**: há?
**area**: área
**arm**: braço
**around**: em volta
**arrest**: prender
**arrive**: chegar
**as**: como
**as...as**: tão...como
**ask**: perguntar, pedir
**as many...as**: tantos...quanto
**ask questions**: faça perguntas
**assistant**: assistente, auxiliar
**as well**: assim como
**at**: em, perto de, junto de
**at home**: em casa
**at night**: à noite
**at present**: atualmente
**at the**: no, na, nos, nas
**atmosphere**: atmosfera
**attend**: frequentar
**attentive**: atento
**attentively**: atentamente
**attract**: atrair
**average**: média
**avoid**: evitar
**aware**: atento
**away**: longe

**B**

**baby**: bebê

**back**: traseiro; atrás, detrás
**backbone**: espinha dorsal
**bacon**: toucinho defumado
**bad**: ruim, mau
**bag**: sacola, mala
**bait**: isca
**baker**: padeiro
**baker's**: padaria
**bank**: banco; margem
**bar graph**: gráfico em barras
**barbecue**: churrasco
**barber**: barbeiro
**barber's**: barbearia
**barrier**: barreira
**basket**: cesta
**basketball**: basquetebol, bola ao cesto
**bath**: banho
**be**: ser, estar, esteja, seja
**be aware**: esteja atento
**beach**: praia
**bean**: feijão
**bear**: urso
**beard**: barba
**beautiful**: bonito
**beauty**: beleza
**because**: porque, por causa de
**become**: tornar-se
**bed**: cama
**bee**: abelha
**been**: sido, estado
**beer**: cerveja

**before**: antes de
**began**: começou
**begin**: começar
**beginning**: começo; começando
**behind**: atrás
**being**: ser (substantivo); sendo
**believe**: acreditar
**belong**: pertencer
**below**: abaixo, debaixo, embaixo de
**belt**: cinto
**beside**: ao lado de
**besides**: além de
**best**: melhor (superlativo)
**better**: melhor (comparativo)
**between**: entre
**big**: grande
**bigger**: maior
**bike**: bicicleta
**bill**: nota, conta
**billion**: bilhão
**bird**: pássaro
**bird watching**: observação dos pássaros
**birth**: nascimento
**birthday**: aniversário
**biscuit**: biscoito
**bite**: morder
**bit**: mordeu
**black**: preto
**blackboard**: lousa
**blind**: cego
**blond**: louro

**blue**: azul
**boat**: barco
**bold**: corajoso
**boldly**: corajosamente
**body**: corpo
**bookseller**: vendedor de livros
**born**: nascido
**borrow**: pedir emprestado
**both**: ambos
**bottle**: garrafa
**bought**: comprou
**box**: caixa
**brake**: breque
**branch**: galho
**Brazilian music**: música brasileira
**bread**: pão
**break**: quebrar
**breakfast**: desjejum, café da manhã
**breath**: respiração
**breathe**: respirar
**bridge**: ponte
**bright**: brilhante
**brilliant**: brilhante
**bring**: trazer, levar
**bring together**: juntar, unir, aproximar
**broke**: quebrou
**brother**: irmão
**brought**: trouxe, trouxeram
**brown**: marrom, castanho
**brush**: escova, pincel
**build**: construir

**building:** construção, edifício; construindo
**bus station:** estação de ônibus
**bush fence:** cerca de arbusto
**business:** negócio
**busy:** ocupado, atarefado
**but:** mas
**butcher:** açougueiro
**butcher's:** açougue
**butter:** manteiga
**butterfly:** borboleta
**button:** botão
**buy:** comprar
**by:** por, de
**by bus:** de ônibus
**by means of:** por meio de

## C
**cabbage:** repolho
**cage:** gaiola
**cake:** bolo
**calculator:** máquina calculadora
**call:** chamar, telefonar
**called:** chamado
**came:** veio, vieram
**camp:** acampamento; acampar
**campaign:** campanha
**camping:** acampamento
**can:** pode, podem, podemos; lata
**canary:** canário
**candy:** bala, doce
**cane:** caniço

**canned food:** alimento enlatado
**cannot:** não pode, não podem
**cap:** boné; tampa
**capable:** capaz
**cards:** baralho, cartas
**care:** cuidado
**careful:** cuidadoso
**carefully:** cuidadosamente
**carnation:** cravo
**carpenter:** carpinteiro
**carrot:** cenoura
**carry:** carregar
**castle:** castelo
**catch:** pegar, apanhar
**caught:** pegou, peguei
**cause:** causa; causar, provocar
**ceiling:** teto, forro
**cellar:** adega, porão
**celebrate:** comemorar
**certain:** certo
**certainly:** certamente
**chance:** chance, probabilidade
**change:** trocar, mudar
**character:** caráter, personagem
**cheap:** barato
**check:** verificar
**cheese:** queijo
**chemist:** farmacêutico
**chicken:** frango
**child:** criança
**children:** crianças, filhos

**choose**: escolher
**chorus**: coro
**Christian**: cristão
**christen**: batizar
**Christmas**: Natal
**church**: igreja
**cigarette**: cigarro
**circus**: circo
**city**: cidade
**classmate**: colega de classe
**classroom**: sala de aula
**clay**: barro
**clean**: limpar; limpo
**cleaner**: limpador, aspirador de pó
**clear**: claro
**clerk**: empregado de loja, balconista
**climb**: subir
**climbing**: escalada
**clock**: relógio
**cloth**: pano
**clothes**: roupas
**clothes hanger**: cabide
**clothing**: vestuário
**clown**: palhaço
**clue**: dica
**clutch**: embreagem
**coast**: costa
**coat**: paletó, casaco
**code**: código
**coffee**: café
**coin**: moeda

**cold**: frio, resfriado, gripe
**collect**: reunir, ajuntar, recolher
**collecting**: colecionando
**color**: cor
**comb**: pente
**come**: vir
**come back**: voltar
**come in**: entrar
**comfortable**: confortável
**command**: comandar
**common**: comum
**comparison**: comparação
**compete**: competir
**complain**: queixar-se
**consider**: considerar
**considered**: considerado
**controlled**: controlado
**cook**: cozinhar; cozinheiro
**cool**: frio
**cooler**: mais frio
**copper**: cobre
**corn**: milho, grão, cereal
**cornflakes**: flocos de milho
**correct**: corrigir; correto
**cost**: custar
**could**: pôde, podia
**country**: país, campo, região
**couple**: casal
**course**: curso
**cousin**: primo
**cover**: cobrir; tampa, cobertura

**cow**: vaca
**crowd**: multidão
**crawl**: arrastar-se
**cream**: creme
**cross**: cruzar; cruz
**cup**: xícara
**cupboard**: armário de cozinha
**cure**: cura
**custom**: costume
**customer**: freguês
**cut**: cortar
**cutting**: cortante; cortando
**cuttlefish**: molusco, siba
**cycle**: andar de bicicleta
**cycling**: ciclismo

**D**
**dad**: pai
**daily**: diário
**daisy**: margarida
**dam**: represa, barragem
**damaged**: danificado
**dangerous**: perigoso
**dark**: escuro
**date**: data, encontro
**daughter**: filha
**day**: dia
**day before yesterday**: anteontem
**dead**: morto
**deal**: quantidade
**death**: morte

**deck of cards**: baralho de cartas, baralho
**deep**: profundo, fundo
**deer**: veado
**definite**: definido
**deliver**: entrega; entregar
**dentist's**: consultório dentário
**deny**: negar
**depend on**: depender de
**deprive**: privar
**deputy**: deputado
**desk**: carteira
**desperate**: desesperado
**destroy**: destruir
**develop**: desenvolver
**devour**: devorar
**diamond card**: naipe de ouro
**die**: morrer
**difficult**: difícil
**difficulty**: dificuldade
**dig**: cavar
**dinner**: jantar
**dirty**: sujo
**disappear**: desaparecer
**discharge**: descarregar
**discovery**: descoberta
**disease**: doença
**dish**: travessa
**dislike**: não gostar, desgostar
**do**: fazer
**doctor**: médico
**doctor's**: consultório médico

**dog**: cachorro
**doing**: fazendo
**doll**: boneca
**done**: feito
**donkey**: burro
**door**: porta
**doorbell**: campainha
**doubt**: dúvida
**down**: para baixo
**drank**: bebeu
**draw**: desenhar, traçar
**drawing**: desenho; desenhando
**dream**: sonhar
**dress**: vestir; vestido
**drew**: desenhou
**drink**: beber
**drive**: dirigir
**driver**: motorista
**drug**: droga, remédio
**drugstore**: drogaria
**dry**: seco; secar
**duck**: pato
**during**: durante

E
**each**: cada
**eager**: ávido
**eagle**: águia
**ear**: orelha, ouvido
**early**: cedo
**early times**: tempos antigos

**earn**: ganhar
**Earth**: Terra
**east**: leste
**easy**: fácil
**eat**: comer
**eaten**: comido
**editor**: editor
**education**: educação, instrução, ensino
**eel**: enguia
**egg**: ovo
**either**: também
**electrical**: elétrico
**electrician**: eletricista
**embroidery**: bordado
**encourage**: encorajar
**end**: fim
**ending**: final
**enemy**: inimigo
**engineer**: engenheiro
**England**: Inglaterra
**English**: inglês
**enjoy**: desfrutar, apreciar, gozar, gostar
**enough**: suficiente
**enter**: entrar
**environment**: meio ambiente
**equal**: igual
**erase**: apagar
**especially**: especialmente
**entertain**: entreter
**even**: até
**event**: acontecimento

**evening**: noite
**ever**: sempre, já
**every**: cada, todos
**everybody**: todos
**everyday**: todos os dias, cada dia
**everyone**: cada um, todo mundo
**everything**: tudo, todas as coisas
**everywhere**: em toda parte
**examine**: examinar
**excuse me**: desculpe-me, com licença
**exercise**: exercício; exercitar
**expansive**: expansivo
**expensive**: caro
**explain**: explicar
**explanation**: explicação
**eye**: olho

**F**
**face**: face; enfrentar, encarar
**fact**: fato
**factory**: fábrica
**fail**: fracassar, falhar
**fair**: feira, bonito, leal
**fairly**: lealmente
**fall**: cair
**false**: falso
**falsehood**: falsidade
**far from**: longe de
**farm**: fazenda
**farmer**: fazendeiro
**farthest**: o mais distante

**fast**: rápido
**fat**: gordo
**father**: pai
**fatter**: mais gordo
**fault**: falta
**favorite**: favorito, preferido
**feast**: festa
**feel**: sentir
**feelings**: sentimentos
**feet**: pés
**fell**: caiu
**fellow**: companheiro
**fence**: cerca
**ferocious**: feroz
**few**: poucos
**field**: campo
**finally**: finalmente
**find**: encontrar
**find out**: descubra
**fine**: ótimo
**finger**: dedo
**finish**: terminar
**fire**: fogo
**fireman**: bombeiro
**first**: primeiro
**fish**: peixe
**fisherman**: pescador
**fishing**: pesca; pescando
**fishmonger**: peixeiro
**fitness**: entrar em forma
**flag**: bandeira

**flat**: apartamento
**flies**: voa
**flight**: voo
**flight attendant**: aeromoça
**floor**: andar, assoalho
**flour**: farinha
**flow**: correr, escorrer
**flower**: flor
**flower arranging**: arranjo de flores
**fly**: voar; mosca
**flying fish**: peixe-voador
**folk-song**: canção popular
**follow**: seguir, acompanhar
**fond of**: fã de
**food**: comida, alimento
**foolish**: bobo
**foot**: pé
**for**: para, por
**for her**: para ela
**for him**: para ele
**for them**: para eles, para elas
**for us**: para nós
**forced**: forçado
**forest**: floresta
**forever**: para sempre
**forget**: esquecer
**fork**: garfo
**forty**: quarenta
**found**: encontrou
**fox**: raposa
**frankly**: francamente

**free**: livre
**frequently**: frequentemente
**fresh**: fresco
**Friday**: sexta-feira
**fridge**: geladeira
**fried**: frito
**friend**: amigo
**friendship**: amizade
**from**: de (origem), desde
**from here**: daqui
**fruit juice**: suco de frutas
**full**: cheio (in full: por extenso)
**fun**: brincadeira, divertimento, graça
**funny**: engraçado
**furnish**: fornecer; mobiliar
**furniture**: móveis, mobília

## G

**game**: jogo
**garage**: garagem
**garbage**: lixo
**garbage bin**: lata de lixo
**garden**: jardim
**gardener**: jardineiro
**gardening**: jardinagem
**gas pedal**: acelerador
**gave**: dei
**generally**: geralmente
**generate**: gerar
**gentle**: gentil, educado
**gentleman**: cavalheiro

**German**: alemão
**get**: conseguir, ter, comprar, chegar
**get engaged**: engajar-se, comprometer-se
**get married**: casar
**get up**: levantar
**ghost**: fantasma, espírito
**girl**: menina, moça
**girlfriend**: namorada
**give**: dar
**glad**: contente, satisfeito, alegre
**glass**: vidro, copo
**glue**: cola
**go**: ir
**goat**: cabra
**go out**: sair
**go to bed**: ir dormir
**goal**: gol, fim, objetivo
**goalkeeper**: goleiro
**God**: Deus
**gold**: ouro
**gone out**: saído
**good**: bom
**goose**: ganso
**got married**: casaram
**government**: governo
**grandfather**: avô
**grandmother**: avó
**great**: grande
**green**: verde
**greengrocer**: verdureiro
**greengrocer's**: quitanda

**grew**: cresceu
**ground**: chão, terra
**grow**: crescer
**grow up**: crescer
**guess**: adivinhar
**guitar**: guitarra, violão
**gun**: revólver
**gym**: ginástica; academia

# H

**had**: tinha, teve
**had just arrived**: tinha acabado de chegar
**hair**: cabelo
**hairdresser**: cabeleireira
**half**: meio, metade
**ham**: presunto
**hand**: mão
**handicraft**: trabalho manual, artesanato
**handsome**: bonito, elegante
**happen**: acontecer
**happily**: felizmente
**happiness**: felicidade
**happy**: feliz
**hard**: duro, árduo, difícil, com afinco
**hare**: lebre
**harmful**: prejudicial
**harvest**: colheita
**has**: tem
**has just pulled**: acabou de puxar
**hat**: chapéu
**hate**: odiar, detestar

**have:** ter
**have a look:** dar uma olhada
**have to:** ter de
**headache:** dor de cabeça
**health:** saúde
**healthy:** saudável
**hear:** ouvir
**heaviest:** o mais pesado
**heavy:** pesado
**held:** segurou
**held a feast:** realizou uma festa
**help:** ajudar; ajuda, socorro
**hen:** galinha
**her:** dela, a, lhe, seu(s), sua(s)
**here:** aqui
**hid:** escondeu
**hidden:** escondido
**hide:** esconder
**high:** alto
**higher:** mais alto
**him:** o, lhe
**himself:** ele mesmo
**his:** dele, seu(s), sua(s)
**history:** história
**hobby:** passatempo
**hogpen:** chiqueiro
**hold:** segurar
**holiday:** feriado, férias
**holidays:** férias
**home:** casa, lar
**homework:** tarefa de casa

**honey:** mel
**hook:** anzol
**hope:** esperança
**horse:** cavalo
**hot:** quente
**hot dog:** cachorro-quente
**hotter:** mais quente
**house:** casa
**house-agent:** corretor de imóveis
**how:** como
**How about...?:** com relação a...?
**How about you?:** E com relação a você?
**How are you?:** Como vai você?
**how far:** a que distância
**how high:** que altura
**how long:** quanto tempo, que comprimento
**how many:** quantos
**how much:** quanto
**how often:** com que frequência
**how old:** que idade
**how quickly:** com que rapidez
**however:** entretanto
**hug:** abraçar
**humming bird:** beija-flor
**hundred:** cem
**hunger:** fome
**hungry:** faminto, com fome
**hungrily:** avidamente
**hunting:** caça; caçando
**hurt:** ferir, machucar
**husband:** marido

**hut**: cabana, barraca

**I**

**I**: eu
**I was born**: eu nasci
**ice**: gelo
**ice cream**: sorvete
**idea**: ideia
**if**: se
**I have just received**: eu acabei de receber
**ill**: doente
**illiteracy**: analfabetismo
**illness**: doença
**I'm**: eu sou, eu estou
**I'm going**: eu vou, eu estou indo
**I'm sorry**: sinto muito
**in**: em
**include**: incluir
**increase**: aumentar
**incredible**: incrível, inacreditável
**Indian**: índio, indígena, indiano
**indicate**: indicar
**injury**: ferimento
**in order to**: afim de
**inquire**: inquirir, perguntar
**insist on**: insistir em
**inspector**: inspetor
**instead of**: em lugar de, em vez de
**intend**: pretender
**interesting**: interessante
**internal**: interno

**interview**: entrevista; entrevistar
**introduce**: apresente
**invent**: inventar
**invention**: invenção
**invite**: convidar
**iron**: ferro
**is going**: vai, está indo
**isn't**: não é, não está
**is there...?**: há...?
**it**: ele, ela
**it's**: é, está
**its**: seu(s), sua(s), dele, dela

**J**

**jam**: geleia
**Japan**: Japão
**Japanese**: japonês
**jealous**: invejoso
**jet plane**: avião a jato
**jeweller**: joalheiro
**jewels**: joias
**job**: emprego, trabalho
**joke**: piada, dito engraçado
**joy**: alegria
**juice**: suco
**jump**: pular
**just**: justo, exatamente, bem

**K**

**keep**: manter, conservar, guardar
**key**: chave

**kill**: matar
**kind**: espécie, tipo, bondoso, amável
**kindly**: bondosamente
**king**: rei
**kiss**: beijar; beijo
**kitchen**: cozinha
**kite**: papagaio, pipa
**kite-making**: fabricação de papagaios
**kite-flying**: empinar papagaios
**knew**: soube, sabia, conhecia
**knife**: faca
**knives**: facas
**knock**: bater
**know**: conhecer, saber

**L**

**lack**: falta
**ladder**: escada
**lady**: dama, senhora
**lake**: lago
**land**: terra
**landscape**: paisagem
**language**: linguagem
**lap**: colo
**large**: grande, amplo, largo
**(the) largest**: o maior de todos
**last**: último
**last year**: no ano passado
**late**: tarde, atrasado, recente
**lately**: recentemente
**later**: mais tarde

**lazy**: preguiçoso
**lead**: conduzir
**leader**: chefe, condutor, líder
**leaf**: folha
**learn**: aprender
**(the) least**: o menor número
**leathercraft**: trabalho em couro
**leave**: partir, deixar
**leaves**: folhas
**left**: esquerda, deixou, saiu
**leg**: perna
**leisure**: lazer
**leisure time**: tempo livre, lazer
**lend**: emprestar
**less...than**: menos...do que
**lesson**: lição, aula
**let**: permitir
**let me**: deixe-me, permita-me
**let's see**: vejamos
**letter**: carta; letra
**lettuce**: alface
**liberation**: liberação
**library**: biblioteca
**lie**: mentira; mentir
**life**: vida
**lifestyle**: estilo de vida
**lift**: levantar; elevador
**light**: luz, lâmpada; leve
**lightning-rod**: para-raios
**like**: gostar; como
**line**: linha

**link**: ligar
**linked**: ligado
**listen to**: ouvir
**listener**: ouvinte
**little**: pequeno
**little by little**: pouco a pouco
**live**: viver, morar
**living**: vivo; vivendo
**living-room**: sala de estar
**load**: carga, fardo
**locate**: localizar
**long**: longo
**longer**: mais longo, mais tempo
**look**: olhar, parecer
**look after**: cuidar
**look for**: procurar
**look like**: parecer (aparência)
**lose**: perder
**lost**: perdido
**lot (a lot)**: uma porção; muito
**love**: amar; amor
**loves**: adora
**low**: baixo; abaixo
**lunch**: almoço

**M**

**macaw**: arara
**machine**: máquina
**madam**: madame
**made**: feito
**magazine**: revista

**maid**: empregada
**mail**: correio, correspondência
**main**: principal
**mainly**: principalmente
**maintenance**: conservação, manutenção
**make**: fazer, fabricar; marca
**make-up**: maquiagem
**mall**: shopping center, centro comercial
**mammal**: mamífero
**man**: homem
**manager**: gerente
**manner**: maneira, modo
**many**: muitos
**mark**: nota, marca; marcar
**market**: mercado
**marriage**: casamento
**marry**: casar
**marvelous**: maravilhoso
**match**: partida; fósforo
**mathematics**: matemática
**matter**: matéria, assunto
**mattress**: colchão
**may**: pode, podem
**May**: maio
**mayor**: prefeito
**meadow**: prado, campo
**meal**: refeição
**mean**: significar
**meaning**: significado
**means**: meios
**measure**: medida

**meat**: carne
**mechanic**: mecânico
**medicine**: remédio
**meet**: encontrar
**meeting**: encontro, reunião
**men**: homens
**mention**: mencionar, citar
**merchandise**: mercadoria
**message**: mensagem
**meter**: metro
**mile**: milha
**mice**: ratos
**midday**: meio-dia
**midnight**: meia-noite
**migrate**: migrar
**mile**: milha
**milk**: leite
**milkman**: leiteiro
**mind**: espírito, mente; importar-se
**mine**: meu, minha
**miss**: perder, sentir falta de
**missing**: faltando
**minute**: minuto
**mistake**: erro
**mixed up**: misturado
**modeling**: modelagem
**modesty**: modéstia
**Monday**: segunda-feira
**money**: dinheiro
**monkey**: macaco
**month**: mês

**more**: mais
**more...than**: mais...do que
**morning**: manhã (good morning: bom dia)
**most**: mais (superlativo); maioria
**mother**: mãe
**mountain**: montanha
**mountain climbing**: escalar montanha
**mouse**: rato
**move**: mudar, movimentar
**movies**: cinema
**much**: muito
**murder**: assassinar
**murderer**: assassino
**must**: precisa, precisamos, precisam

**N**
**name**: nome
**nasty**: sujo
**nature**: natureza
**near**: perto de
**nearby**: perto, aqui perto
**need**: precisar
**needle**: agulha
**neighbor**: vizinho
**neighborhood**: vizinhança
**neither**: nem
**nest**: ninho
**Netherlands**: Países Baixos, Holanda
**never**: nunca
**new**: novo

**news**: notícias, novidades
**newsagent**: jornaleiro
**newspaper**: jornal
**next**: próximo
**nice**: bom, bonito, ótimo, "legal"
**night**: noite
**no**: não, nenhum
**Nobel Peace Prize**: Prêmio Nobel da Paz
**no more**: não mais
**nobody**: ninguém
**noise**: barulho
**none**: nenhum
**north**: norte
**Norway**: Noruega
**nose**: nariz
**not so...as**: não tão...quanto
**note**: nota; notar, observar
**notebook**: caderno de anotações, agenda
**nothing**: nada
**noun**: substantivo
**now**: agora
**nowadays**: hoje em dia
**now and then**: de vez em quando
**number**: número
**nurse**: enfermeira
**nut**: noz

# O

**obey**: obedecer
**occasionally**: ocasionalmente
**occupation**: ocupação, profissão
**occupy**: ocupar
**octopus**: polvo
**odd**: estranho
**of**: de
**of course**: naturalmente, certamente
**of them**: deles
**off**: fora
**offer**: oferecer; oferta
**office**: escritório
**often**: frequentemente
**oil**: óleo
**old**: velho
**older**: mais velho
**omit**: omitir
**on**: sobre, em
**one**: um, alguém
**one third**: um terço
**on fire**: em chamas
**only**: somente
**on the**: no, na, nos, nas
**on the left**: à esquerda
**on the right**: à direita
**on time**: a tempo
**open**: abrir
**opinion**: opinião
**opposite**: antônimo, oposto
**or**: ou
**orange juice**: suco de laranja
**orange tree**: laranjeira
**order (in order to)**: a fim de
**ordinary**: ordinário, comum

**organism:** organismo
**organize:** organizar
**origin:** origem
**other:** outro
**our:** nosso(a)
**out:** fora
**out of:** fora de
**outdoor:** do lado de fora, externo
**outside:** do lado de fora
**over:** acima de
**own:** próprio
**owner:** possuidor, dono
**ox, oxen:** boi, bois

P

**pack:** pacote; empacotar
**packet:** pacote, embrulho
**packing:** empacotamento, embalagem
**paint:** pintar; pintura
**painter's brush:** pincel
**painting:** pintura; pintando
**pair:** par
**pair of shoes:** par de sapatos
**paper:** papel; jornal
**parakeet:** periquito
**paralyze:** paralisar
**parcel:** pacote
**parents:** pais
**park:** parque
**parrot:** papagaio (ave)
**part:** parte, acessório

**party:** festa
**pass:** passar
**past:** passado
**patient:** paciente
**pay:** pagar, prestar
**pay attention:** prestar atenção
**peace:** paz
**peach:** pêssego
**peak:** pico
**peanut:** amendoim
**pear:** pera
**pen:** caneta
**pencil:** lápis
**people:** pessoas, povo
**person:** pessoa
**personal:** pessoal
**pet:** animal de estimação
**phone:** telefone; telefonar
**pick:** colher
**picture:** quadro, figura, pintura
**piece:** pedaço, peça
**pig:** porco
**pill:** comprimido
**pilot:** piloto
**pine tree:** pinheiro
**pipe:** cano
**place:** lugar; colocar
**plane:** avião (aeroplane, airplane: avião)
**plant:** planta; plantar
**plate:** prato
**play:** jogar, brincar, tocar instrumento

musical

**player**: jogador

**play the piano**: tocar piano

**please**: por favor

**pleasure**: prazer

**plumbing**: encanamento

**pole**: vara

**police**: polícia

**policeman**: policial

**police station**: delegacia de polícia

**polished**: polido

**polite**: polido, educado

**politician**: político

**polluted**: poluído

**pollution**: poluição

**poor**: pobre

**pop**: popular

**Portuguese**: português

**possible**: possível

**post office**: correio

**postcard**: cartão-postal

**postman**: carteiro

**pound**: libra (peso ou moeda inglesa)

**poverty**: pobreza

**power**: poder, força

**powerful**: poderoso

**practice**: prática; praticar

**precious**: precioso

**predict**: predizer

**prefer**: preferir

**prepare**: preparar

**preserve**: preservar

**press**: pressione, apertar

**pressure**: pressão

**pretty**: bonito

**prey**: presa, caça

**price**: preço

**prince**: príncipe

**princess**: princesa

**print**: imprimir

**printing**: impressão

**proclaim**: proclamar

**profitable**: proveitoso, lucrativo

**protect**: proteger

**public**: público

**pull**: puxar

**pullover**: pulôver

**pupil**: aluno

**Puritans**: puritanos

**purpose**: propósito, finalidade

**purse**: bolsa

**put**: pôr, ponha, colocar

**put out**: apagar

## Q

**quarter**: um quarto, 15 minutos

**question**: pergunta, questão

**quick**: rápido

**quickly**: rapidamente

## R

**radiator**: radiador

**rain:** chuva; chover
**rainbow:** arco-íris
**rainbow fish:** peixe arco-íris
**raise:** criar, cultivar
**raising animals:** criação de animais
**raising plants:** cultivo de plantas
**ran:** correu
**rat:** rato
**reach:** alcançar, conseguir
**read:** ler
**reading:** leitura; lendo
**really:** realmente
**rearrange:** ordenar
**reason:** razão, motivo
**receive:** receber
**recently:** recentemente
**recognize:** reconhecer
**record:** disco, gravação; gravar
**recreation:** recreação
**red:** vermelho
**red heart card:** carta de baralho, naipe copas
**redecorated:** redecorado
**reduce:** reduzir
**refer to:** referir-se a
**region:** região
**regularly:** regularmente
**related:** relacionado
**relation:** relação
**relatives:** parentes
**reliable:** seguro

**remain:** permanecer
**remember:** lembrar-se de, lembrar
**renovated:** reformado
**rent:** alugar
**repair:** consertar
**replace:** recolocar, repor
**report card:** boletim
**reptile:** réptil
**research:** pesquisa
**resist:** resistir
**resource:** recurso
**return:** voltar; volta
**return home:** voltar para casa
**rib:** costela
**rice:** arroz
**rich:** rico
**ride:** andar, cavalgar
**right:** reto, direito, correto
**rights:** direitos
**rigid:** rígido, firme
**ring:** anel; tocar, telefonema
**ring the bell:** tocar a campainha
**ripe:** maduro
**rise up:** levantar-se
**river:** rio
**road:** estrada, rua
**rob:** roubar estabelecimento comercial, instituição, organização
**rock:** rocha, pedra
**role:** função, papel
**roof:** telhado

**room**: sala
**rotten**: estragado, gasto, podre
**round**: redondo
**royal**: real
**rule**: regra
**ruler**: régua
**run**: correr

**S**
**sad**: triste
**sadder**: mais triste
**safe**: cofre
**safety**: segurança
**said**: disse
**sailing**: navegação
**salad**: salada
**sale**: venda
**salesman**: vendedor
**same**: mesmo
**sand**: areia
**satisfied**: satisfeito
**Saturday**: sábado
**sausage**: salsicha, linguiça
**save**: economizar, salvar
**saw**: vi, viu, via
**say**: dizer
**school**: escola, cardume
**school year**: ano letivo
**science**: ciência
**scientist**: cientista
**score**: marcar (esporte)

**Scottish**: escocês
**scrambled**: embaralhado
**screen**: tela
**sculpture**: escultura
**sea**: mar
**season**: estação (ano)
**seat**: assento
**seat belt**: cinto de segurança
**secretary**: secretária
**see**: ver
**sell**: vender
**seller**: vendedor
**send**: enviar, mandar
**sent**: enviou
**separate**: separar
**serious**: sério
**set**: pôr, estabelecer
**settled**: estabelecido
**several**: vários
**sew**: costurar
**shape**: forma
**share**: repartir
**sheep**: ovelha
**shell**: concha
**shellfish**: marisco, molusco de concha
**shine**: brilhar; brilho
**ship**: navio
**shirt**: camisa
**shock**: choque
**shoe**: sapato
**shop**: loja

**short:** curto, baixo
**should take:** deveria tomar
**shoulder:** ombro
**shout:** gritar
**show:** mostrar; espetáculo
**shower:** chuveiro
**shut:** fechar
**sick:** doente
**sigh:** suspiro
**sight:** vista
**sign:** sinal; assinalar, marcar com sinal, assinar
**silly:** bobo
**silver:** prata
**since:** desde
**sing:** cantar
**singer:** cantor, cantora
**sink:** pia, afundar
**sir:** senhor
**sister:** irmã
**sit:** sentar
**sitting:** sentado, sentando
**sixty:** sessenta
**skin:** pele
**skirt:** saia
**sky:** céu
**sleep:** dormir
**sleeping:** dormindo
**slow:** vagaroso
**slowly:** vagarosamente
**small:** pequeno

**smart:** esperto, inteligente
**smell:** cheirar
**smelly:** malcheiroso
**smile:** sorrir; sorriso
**smoke:** fumar; fumaça
**snackbar:** lanchonete
**snake:** cobra
**snow:** neve
**so:** tão; por isso
**soap:** sabão
**sociability:** sociabilidade
**society:** sociedade
**sock:** meia
**soft:** suave, macio
**sold:** vendido
**soldier:** soldado
**solution:** solução
**solve:** resolver
**so many:** tantos
**so much:** tanto
**so that:** de modo que
**some:** alguns, algum, um pouco
**some of them:** alguns deles
**somebody:** alguém
**someone:** alguém
**something:** algo, alguma coisa
**sometimes:** algumas vezes, às vezes
**somewhere:** em algum lugar
**son:** filho
**song:** canto, canção
**soon:** logo

**sorry**: sinto muito, desculpe
**soul**: alma
**soup**: sopa
**source**: fonte, origem
**south**: sul
**space**: espaço
**spaceship**: nave espacial
**spade**: pá
**Spanish**: espanhol
**spare time**: tempo livre, tempo de lazer
**speak**: falar
**speaker**: locutor
**species**: espécie
**speed**: velocidade
**spell**: soletrar
**spend**: gastar, passar
**spinach**: espinafre
**spoil**: estragar
**spot**: ponto
**spread**: espalhar
**spring**: primavera
**square**: praça, largo, quarteirão, quadrado
**squirrel**: esquilo, serelepe
**stadium**: estádio
**stamp**: selo
**stand**: ficar, suportar
**standard**: comum, padrão
**standing**: em pé
**star**: estrela
**starfish**: estrela-do-mar
**start**: começo; começar

**state**: estado
**stationer**: papeleiro
**stay**: ficar
**steak**: filé, bife, fatia de carne
**steal**: roubar (pessoas) – (rob: roubar organizações, bancos etc.)
**steam**: vapor
**steam boat**: barco a vapor
**stick**: colar
**still**: ainda (till: até)
**stole**: roubou
**stolen**: roubado
**stone**: pedra
**stonemason**: pedreiro
**stop**: parar, parada, ponto
**store**: armazenar, loja
**story**: história, conto
**strange**: estranho
**strangly**: estranhamente
**street**: rua
**string**: corda
**strong**: forte
**student**: estudante
**study**: estudar
**stutter**: gaguejar
**stutterer**: gago
**such as**: assim como
**sugar**: açúcar
**suit**: terno, traje
**summer**: verão
**Sunday**: domingo

**sunflower**: girassol
**sunshine**: raio de sol
**sure**: com certeza
**surely**: claro, certamente
**surface**: superfície
**surrounding**: arredor
**survive**: sobreviver
**sweep**: varrer
**sweet**: doce
**sweetener**: adoçante
**swim**: nadar
**swimming**: natação
**switch on**: ligar

**T**
**table**: mesa
**tail**: rabo
**take**: pegar, tomar, levar
**take a look**: dar uma olhada
**take a trip**: fazer uma viagem
**take care**: cuidar
**take part**: tomar parte
**talk**: conversar; conversa, palestra
**tall**: alto
**tame**: manso, domesticar
**taught**: ensinado
**tea**: chá
**teach**: ensinar
**teacher**: professor, professora
**team**: time
**technology**: tecnologia

**teeth**: dentes
**tell**: contar, dizer
**tender**: terno, amoroso
**tenderly**: ternamente
**tennis**: tênis
**terrarium**: viveiro de animais terrestres
**than**: do que (comparação)
**thank**: agradecer, agradeço
**Thanksgiving**: Dia de Ação de Graças
**that**: que, aquele, aquela
**that is**: isso é
**the most**: o mais
**theater**: teatro
**their**: deles, delas
**them**: a eles, lhes, os, as
**then**: então, depois
**there**: lá, ali
**there are**: há (plural)
**there is**: há (singular)
**there was**: havia (singular)
**there were**: havia (plural)
**these**: estes, estas
**thick**: grosso, espesso
**thief**: ladrão (thieves: ladrões)
**thin**: fino, magro
**thing**: coisa
**think**: pensar
**thirsty**: com sede
**thirty**: trinta
**this**: este, esta, isto
**those**: aqueles, aquelas

**thousand**: mil, milhar
**through**: através de
**Thursday**: quinta-feira
**ticket**: bilhete, passagem
**tiger**: tigre
**till**: até
**time**: tempo
**times**: vezes, tempos
**time line**: linha do tempo
**tire**: pneu
**tired**: cansado
**to**: para, a
**to her**: para ela
**to him**: para ele
**toast**: torrada
**today**: hoje
**together**: juntos
**toilet**: banheiro
**told**: disse
**tolerate**: tolerar
**tomato**: tomate
**tomorrow**: amanhã
**ton**: tonelada
**tonight**: esta noite
**too**: demais, também
**too much**: demais
**took**: tomou, levou
**tooth**: dente
**topaz**: topázio
**towel**: toalha
**tower**: torre

**town**: cidade
**toy**: brinquedo
**traditional**: tradicional
**train**: trem
**travel**: viajar; viagem
**treasure**: tesouro
**treat**: tratar
**tree**: árvore
**trip**: viagem
**trousers**: calça
**trout**: truta
**truck**: caminhão
**true**: verdadeiro
**truth**: verdade
**try**: tentar, experimentar
**Tuesday**: terça-feira
**tune**: melodia
**turn off**: desligar
**turn on**: ligar
**turkey**: peru
**turtle**: tartaruga
**twenty**: vinte
**twice**: duas vezes
**twin**: gêmeo
**type**: tipo
**typist**: datilógrafo

**U**

**under**: debaixo
**understand**: compreender
**unemployed**: desempregado

**unfit**: despreparado, fora de forma
**unfortunately**: infelizmente
**unhappiness**: infelicidade
**unscramble**: desembaralhar
**until**: até
**up**: para cima
**upstairs**: para cima, em cima, no andar de cima
**us**: nos, nós
**use**: usar
**usually**: geralmente

## V
**vacation**: férias
**valley**: vale
**varied**: variado
**various**: vários
**vegetable**: legume
**verse**: verso
**vertebrate**: vertebrado
**very**: muito
**very much**: muitíssimo
**very well**: muito bem
**vinegar**: vinagre
**virtue**: virtude
**voice**: voz
**vote**: votar

## W
**wage**: salário
**wait**: esperar

**waiter**: garçom
**waitress**: garçonete
**wake up**: acordar, levantar-se
**walk**: caminhar
**wallet**: carteira de dinheiro
**want**: desejar, querer
**war**: guerra
**wardrobe**: guarda-roupa
**warm**: quente
**was**: era, estava, foi
**was born**: nasceu, nasci
**was built**: foi construído
**was painted**: foi pintado
**wash**: lavar, regar
**washing machine**: máquina de lavar
**waste**: lixo, resíduos industriais
**watch**: assistir a; relógio
**water**: água
**waterfall**: queda de água, catarata
**watermelon**: melancia
**way**: caminho, modo, maneira, pista
**weak**: fraco
**weakly**: fracamente
**wealth**: riqueza
**wear**: usar (vestir roupas)
**weather**: tempo (condições meteorológicas)
**web**: rede
**Wednesday**: quarta-feira
**week**: semana
**weekend**: fim de semana

**weigh**: pesar
**welcome**: bem-vindo
**well**: bem
**well-meaning**: bem-intencionado
**went**: foi
**went away**: foi embora
**went out**: saiu
**were**: eram, estavam, foram
**whale**: baleia
**what**: o que, qual
**what about**: com relação a
**what kind**: que tipo
**What's the matter?**: De que se trata? Qual é o problema?
**What time is it**: Que horas são?
**wheat flour**: farinha de trigo
**wheel**: roda
**when**: quando
**When were you born?**: Quando você nasceu?
**where**: onde
**which**: que, qual
**while**: enquanto
**white**: branco
**who**: que, quem
**Who are you?**: Quem é você?
**whole**: todo
**whom**: a quem, de quem, para quem
**whose**: cujo
**why**: por que
**why not**: por que não

**wide**: amplo
**wife**: esposa
**wild**: selvagem
**will**: vontade; forma auxiliar dos verbos no futuro do presente
**will be**: serei
**win**: vencer, ganhar
**window**: janela
**wine**: vinho
**winter**: inverno
**wire**: fio
**wisdom**: sabedoria
**wish**: desejo; desejar
**with**: com
**with her**: com ela
**with us**: conosco
**without**: sem
**wolf**: lobo
**woman**: mulher
**won**: ganhasse, ganhou, venceu
**wonder**: maravilha
**wonderful**: maravilhoso
**wood**: madeira, mata
**word**: palavra
**world**: mundo (all over the world: no mundo todo)
**work**: trabalho; trabalhar, funcionar
**working**: trabalhando
**worm**: minhoca, verme
**worse**: pior (comparativo)
**worst**: pior (superlativo)

**worth**: valor

**would like**: gostaria

**wrist**: pulso

**write**: escrever, escreva

**writer**: escritor

**wrong**: errado

## Y

**year**: ano

**yesterday**: ontem

**yet**: ainda

**you**: você, vocês

**yoghurt**: iogurte

**young**: jovem, novo

**younger**: mais jovem

**your**: seu (adjetivo possessivo)

**you're welcome**: de nada (em agradecimentos)

**yours**: seu (pronome possessivo)

## Z

**ZIP Code**: CEP